ADULT COLORING BOOKS

MANDALA DESIGNS

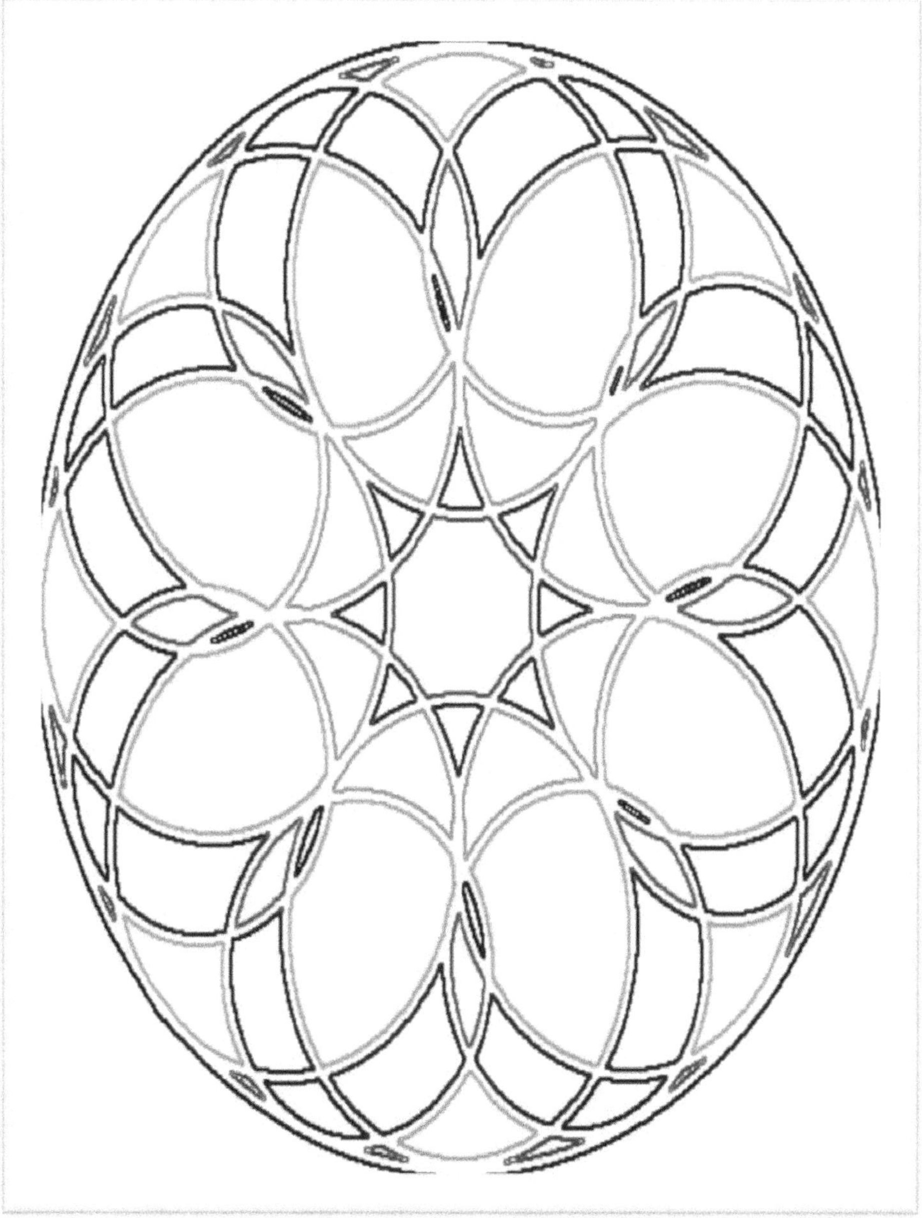

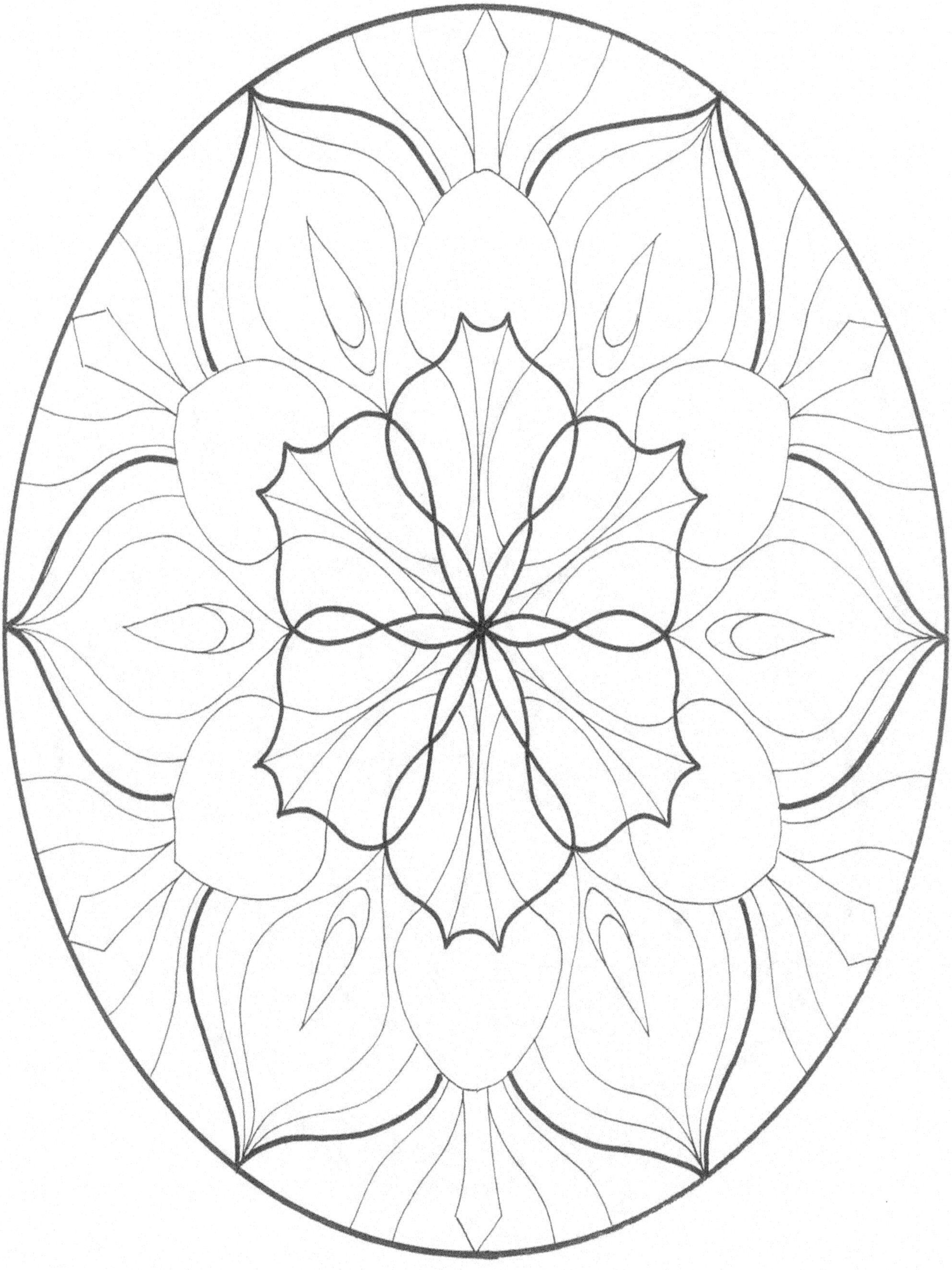

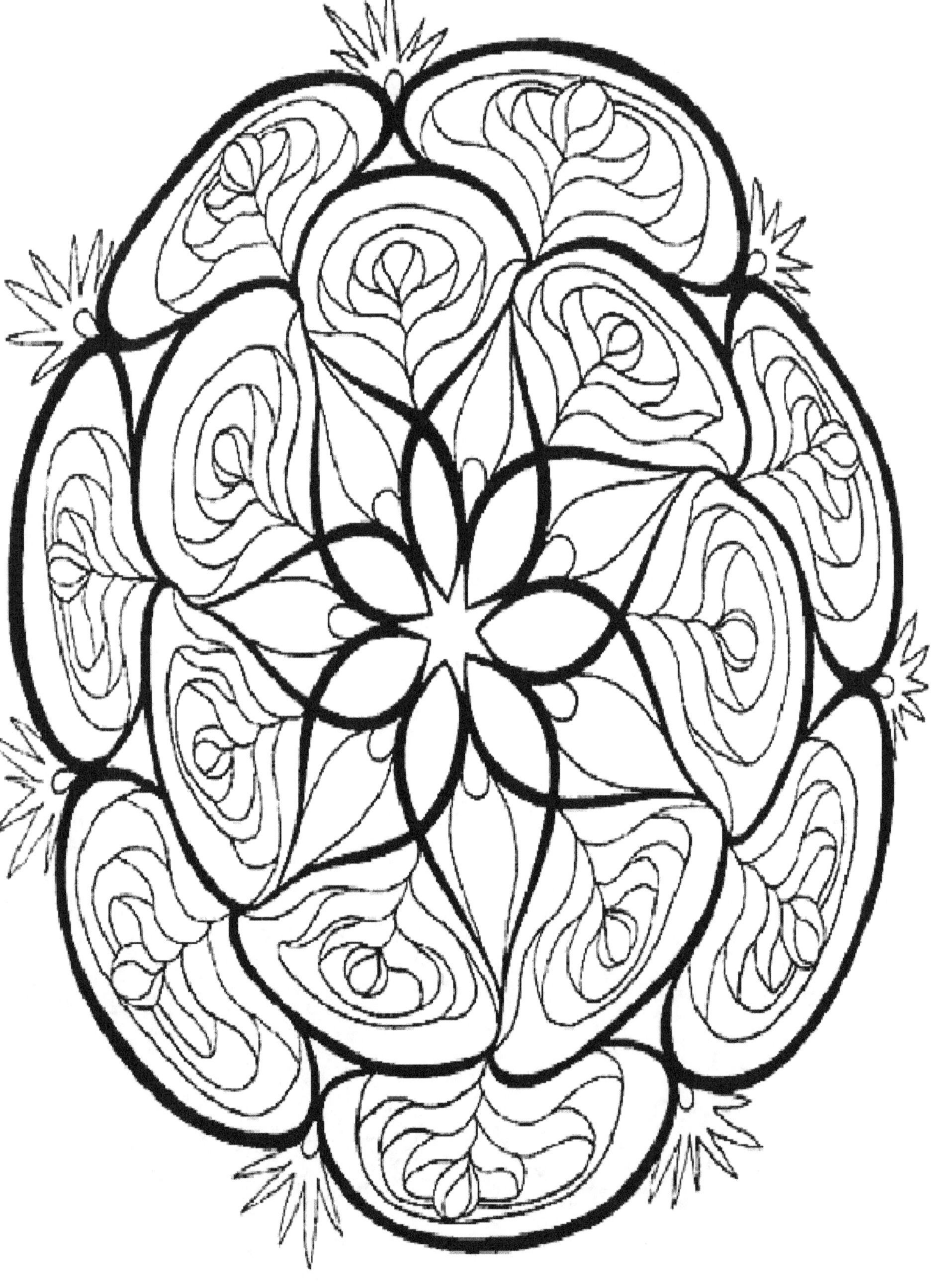

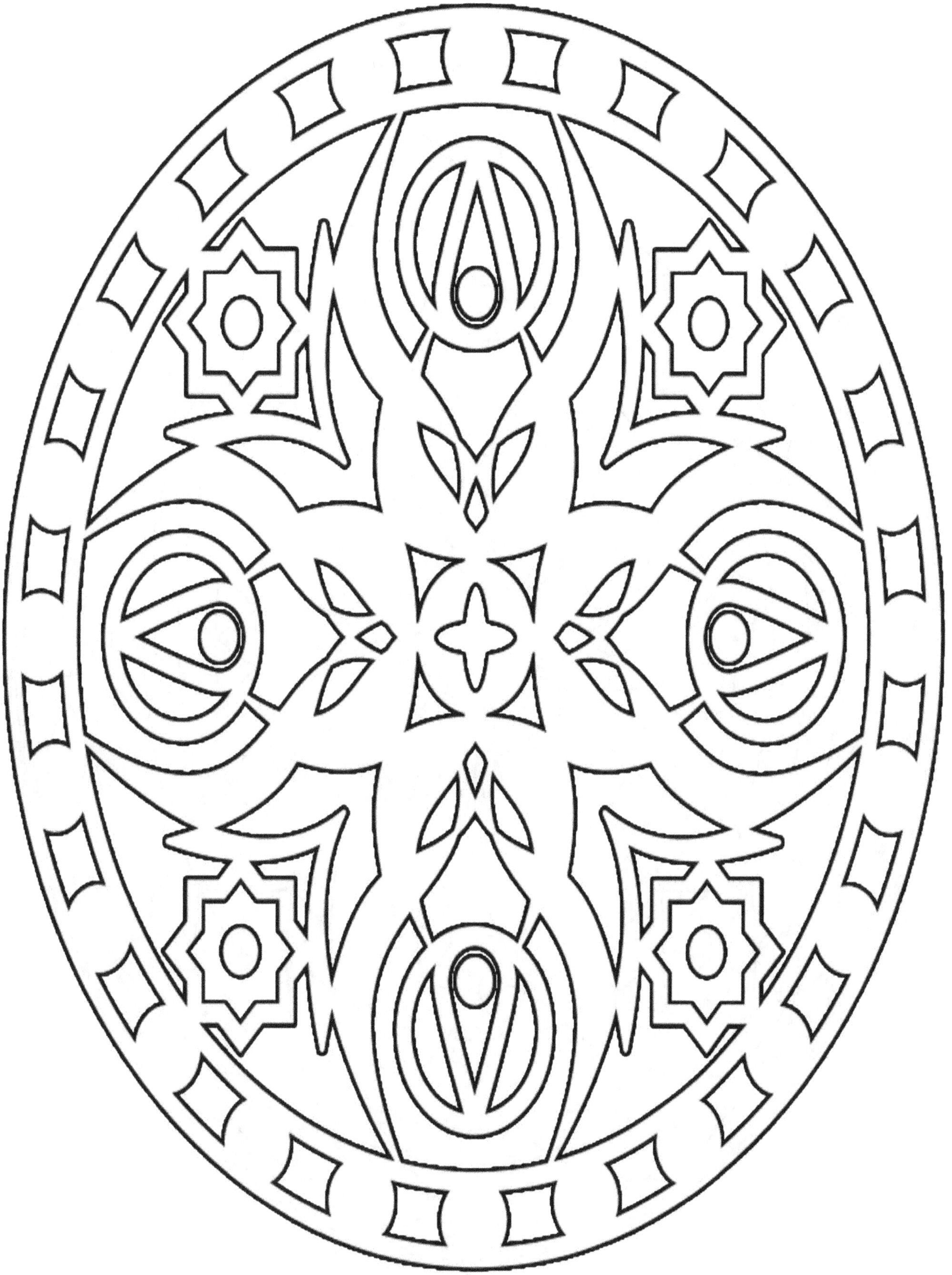

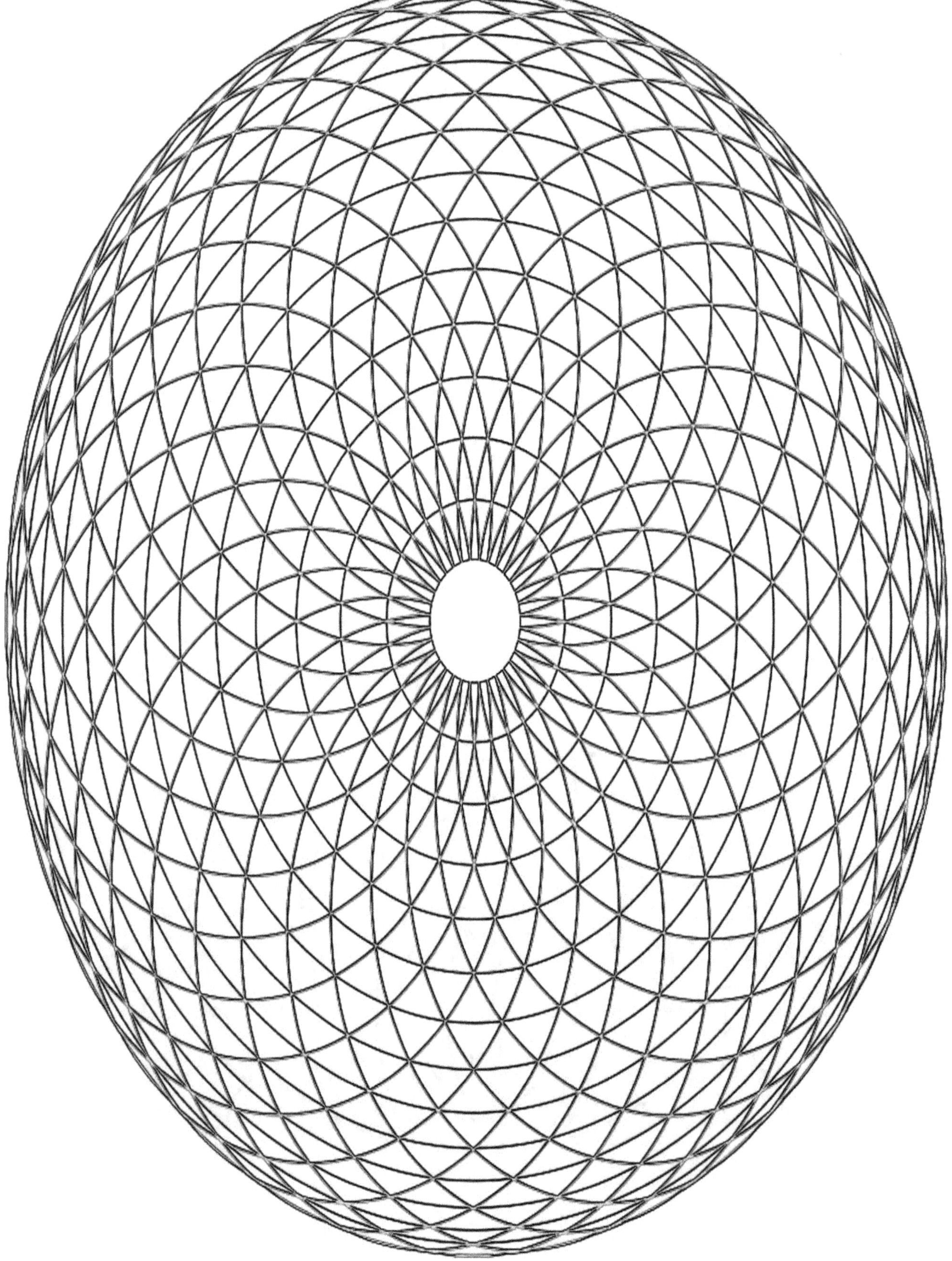

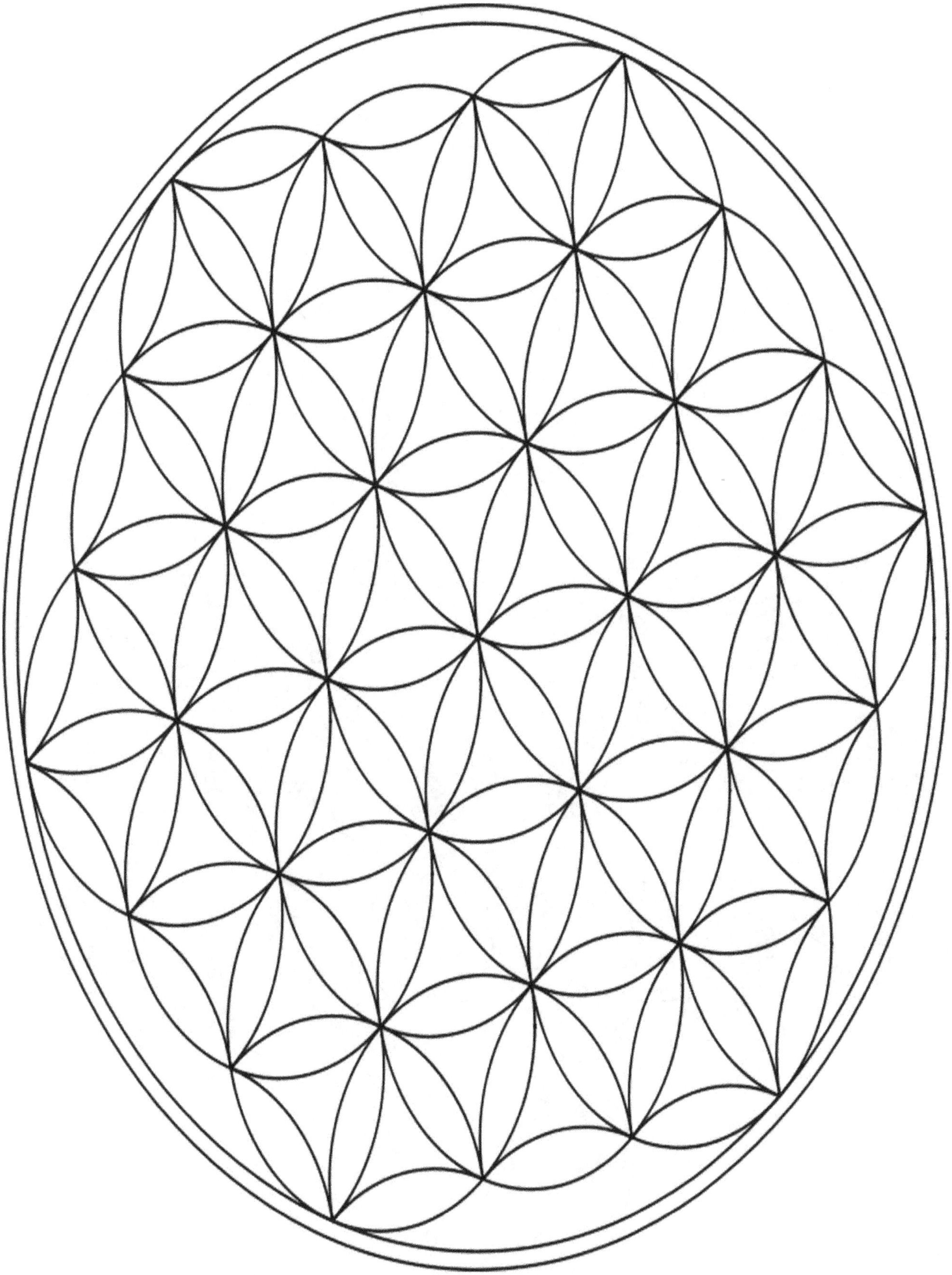

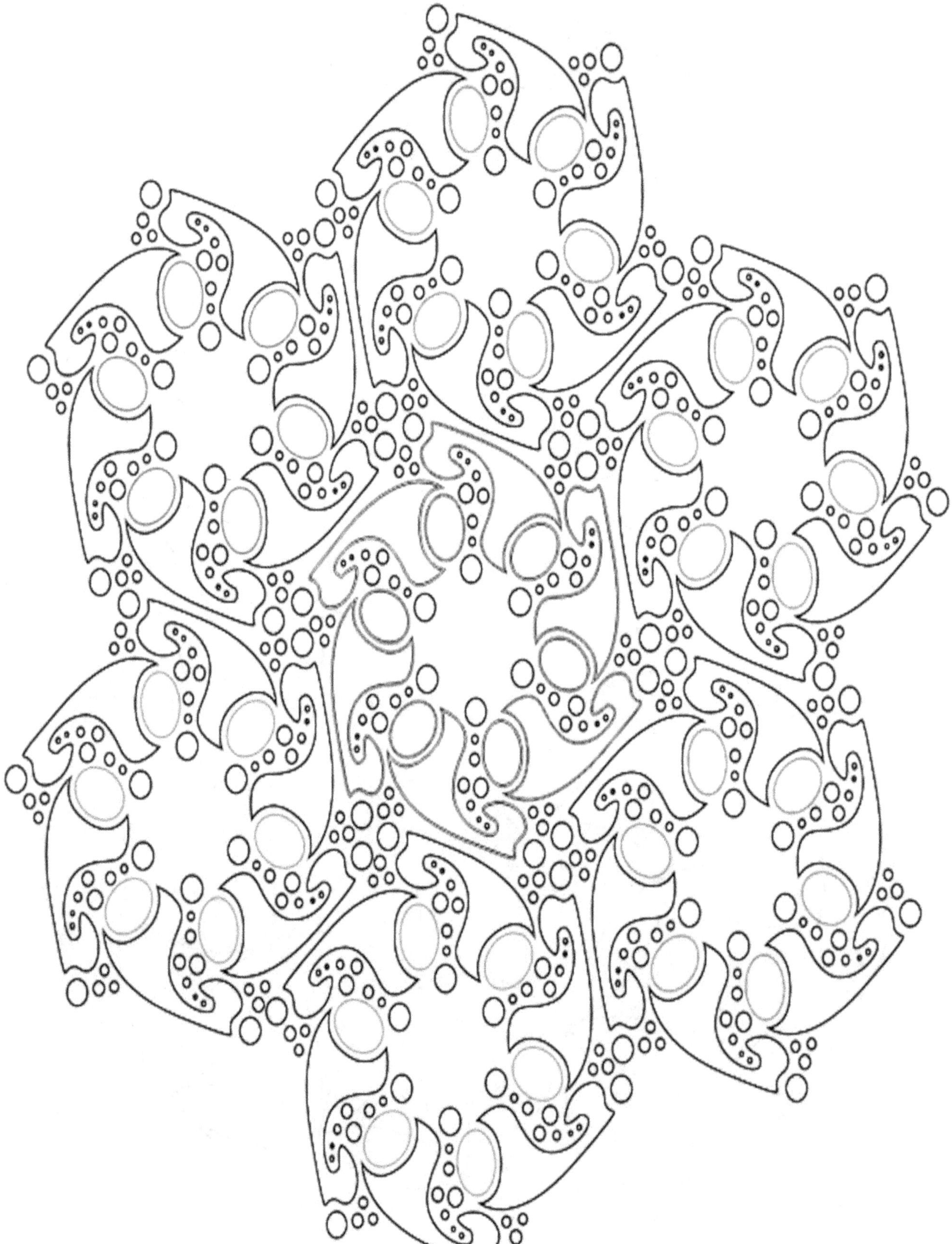

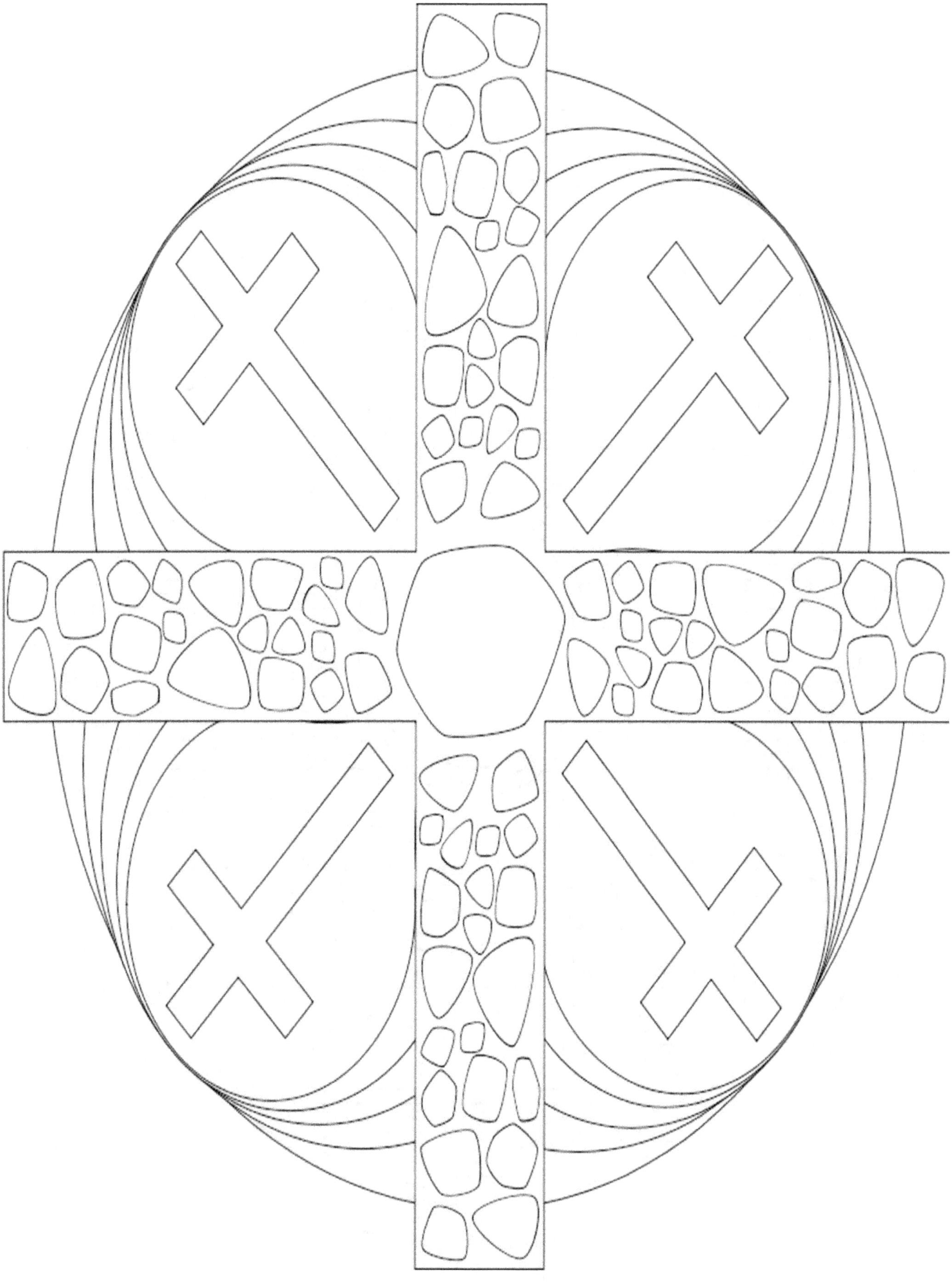

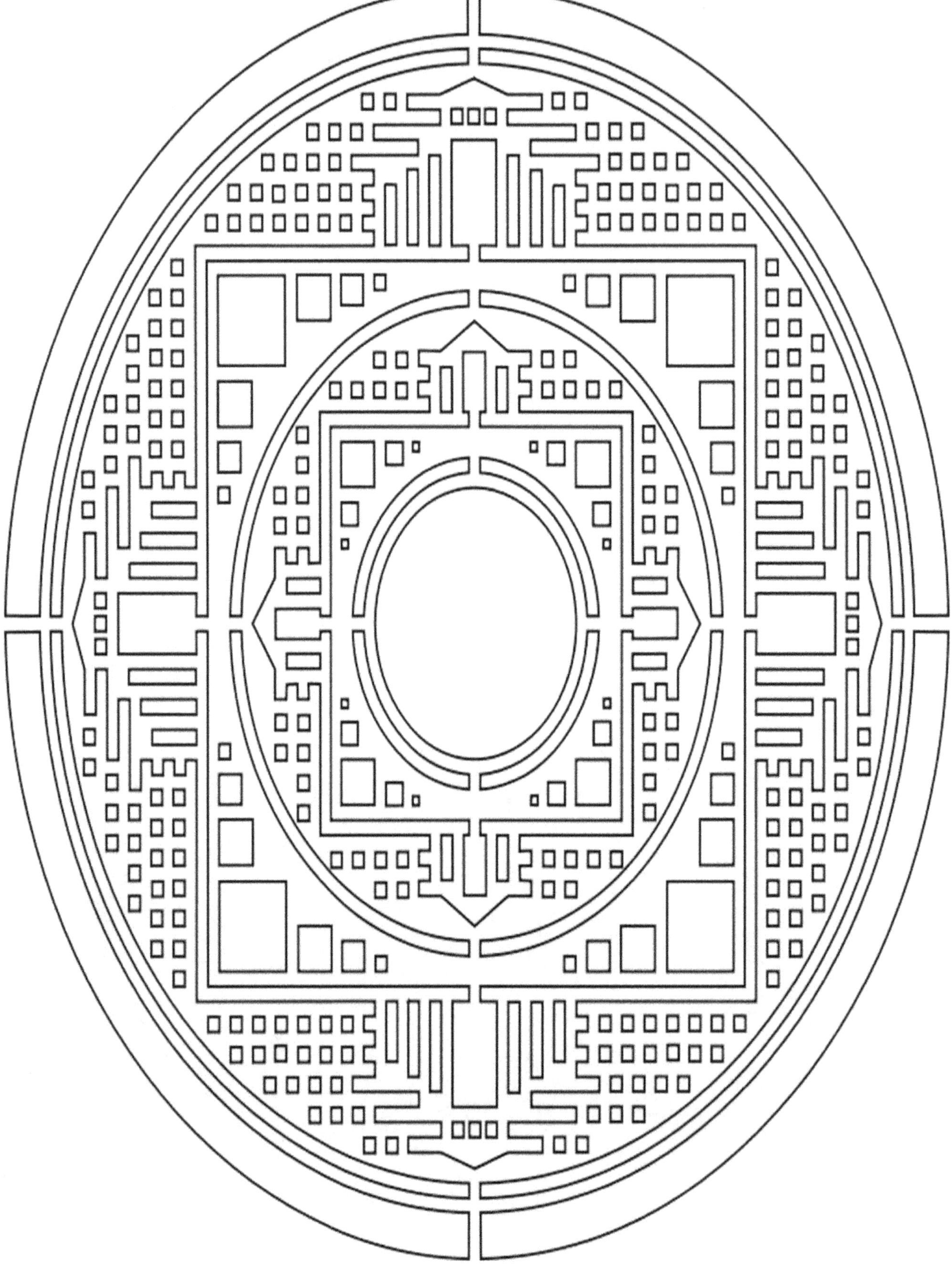

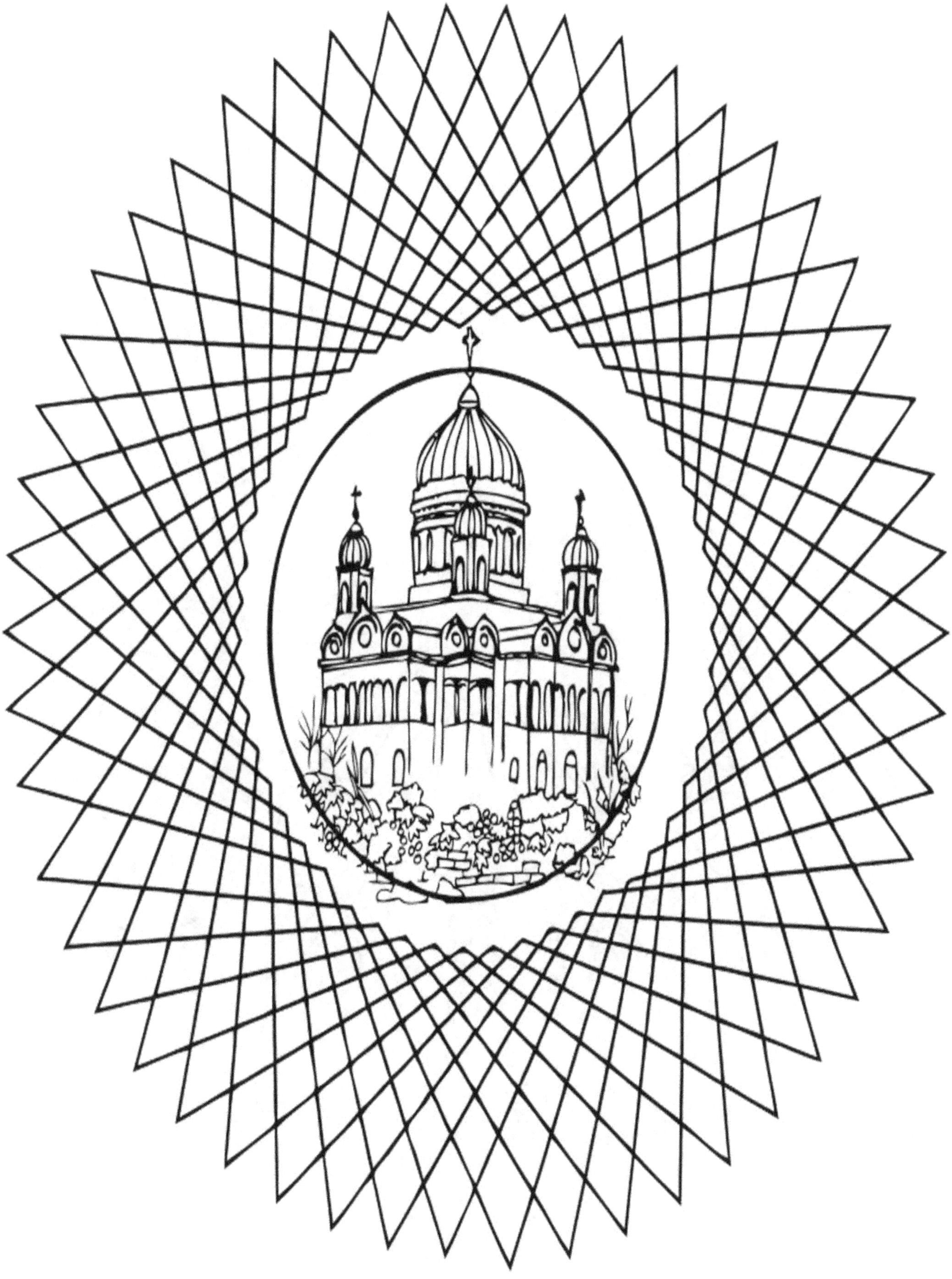

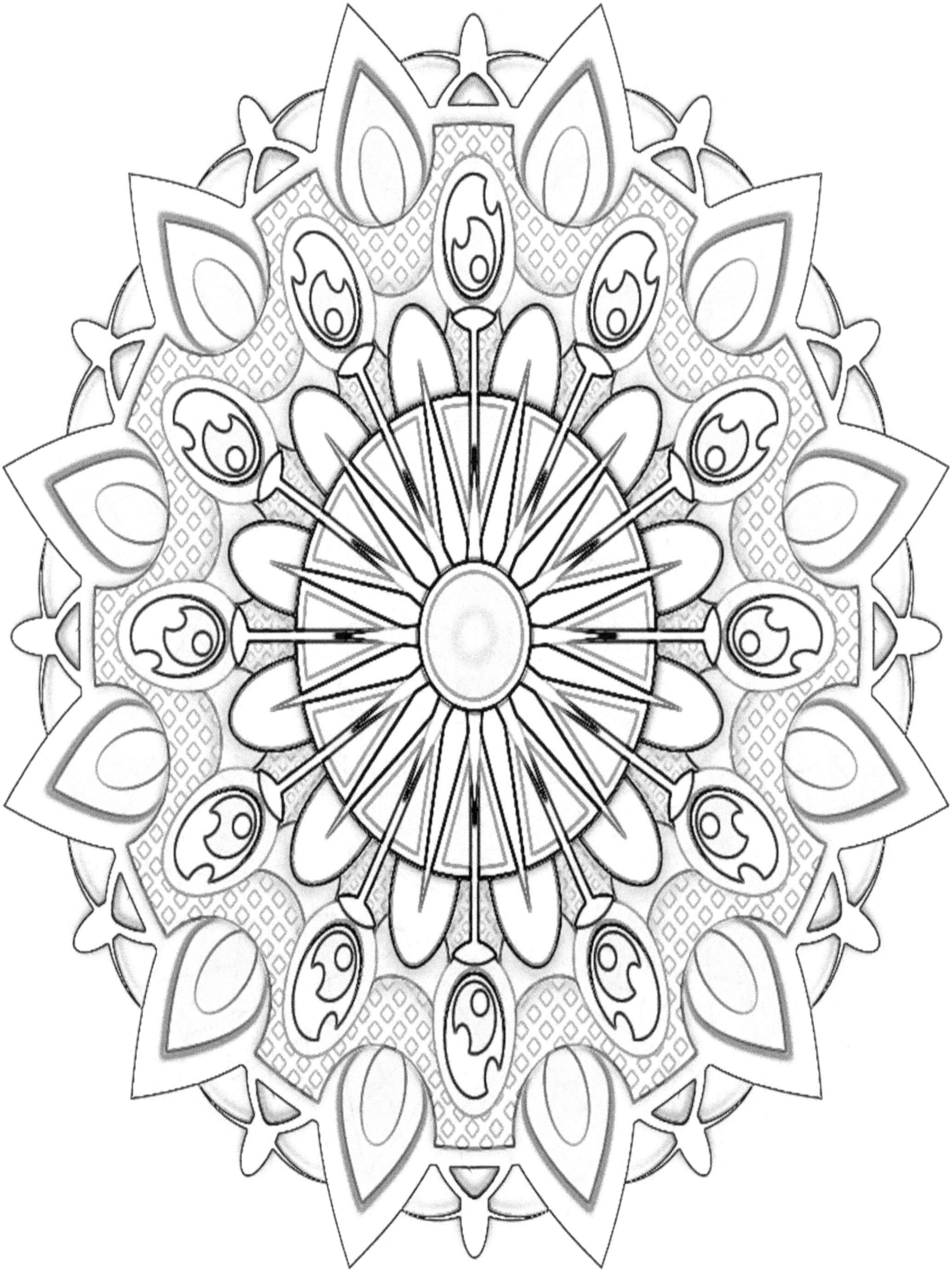

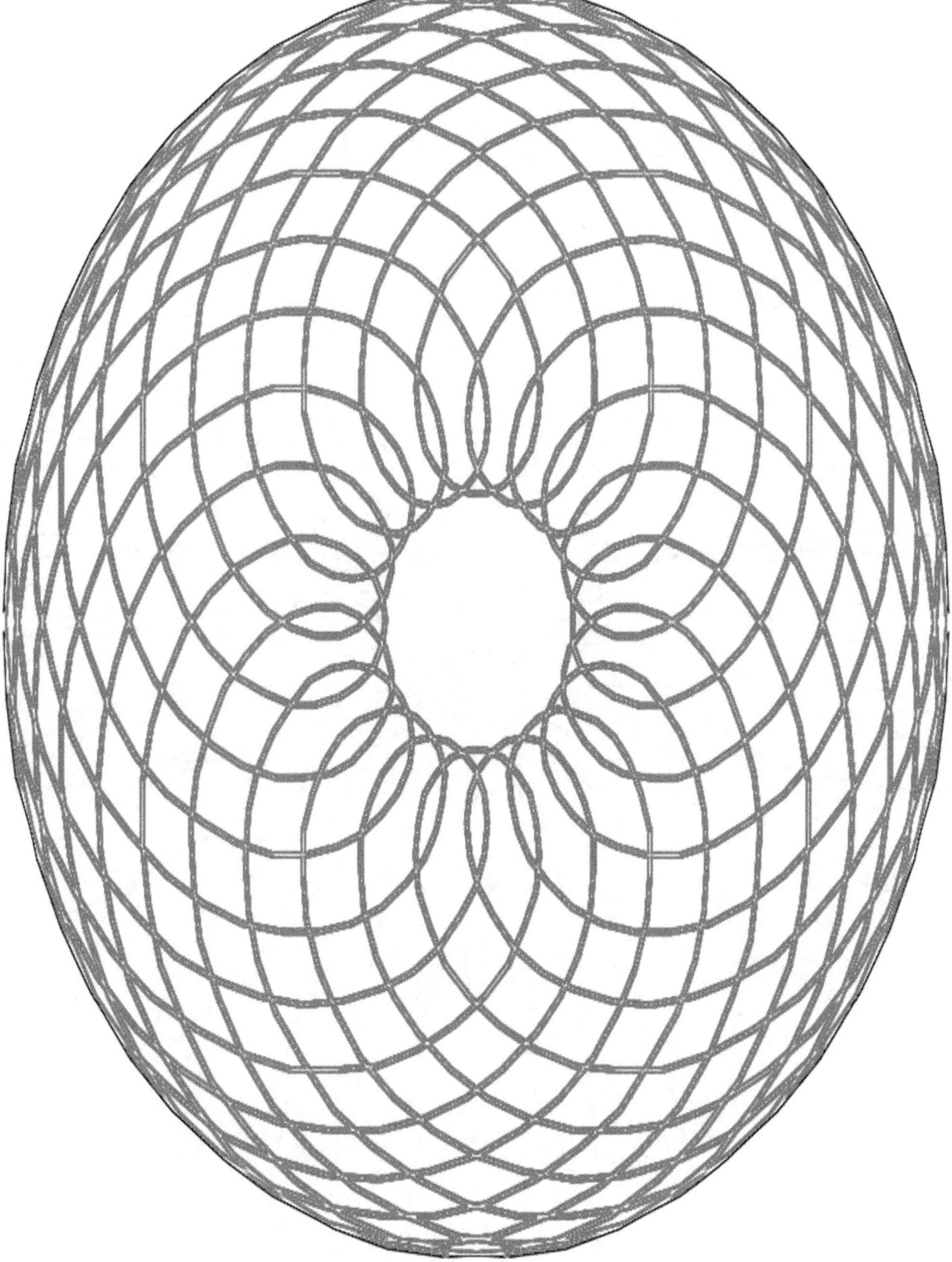

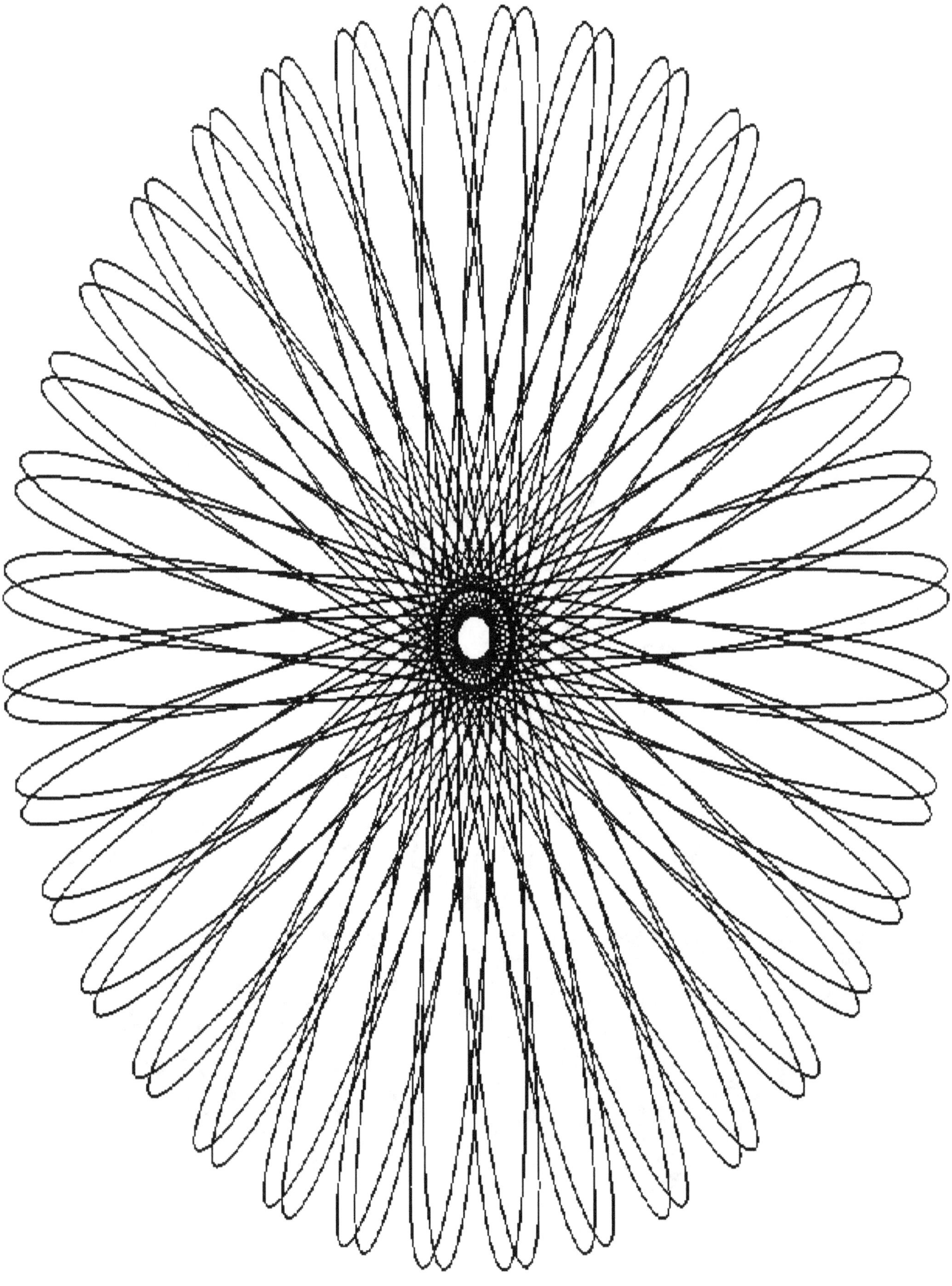

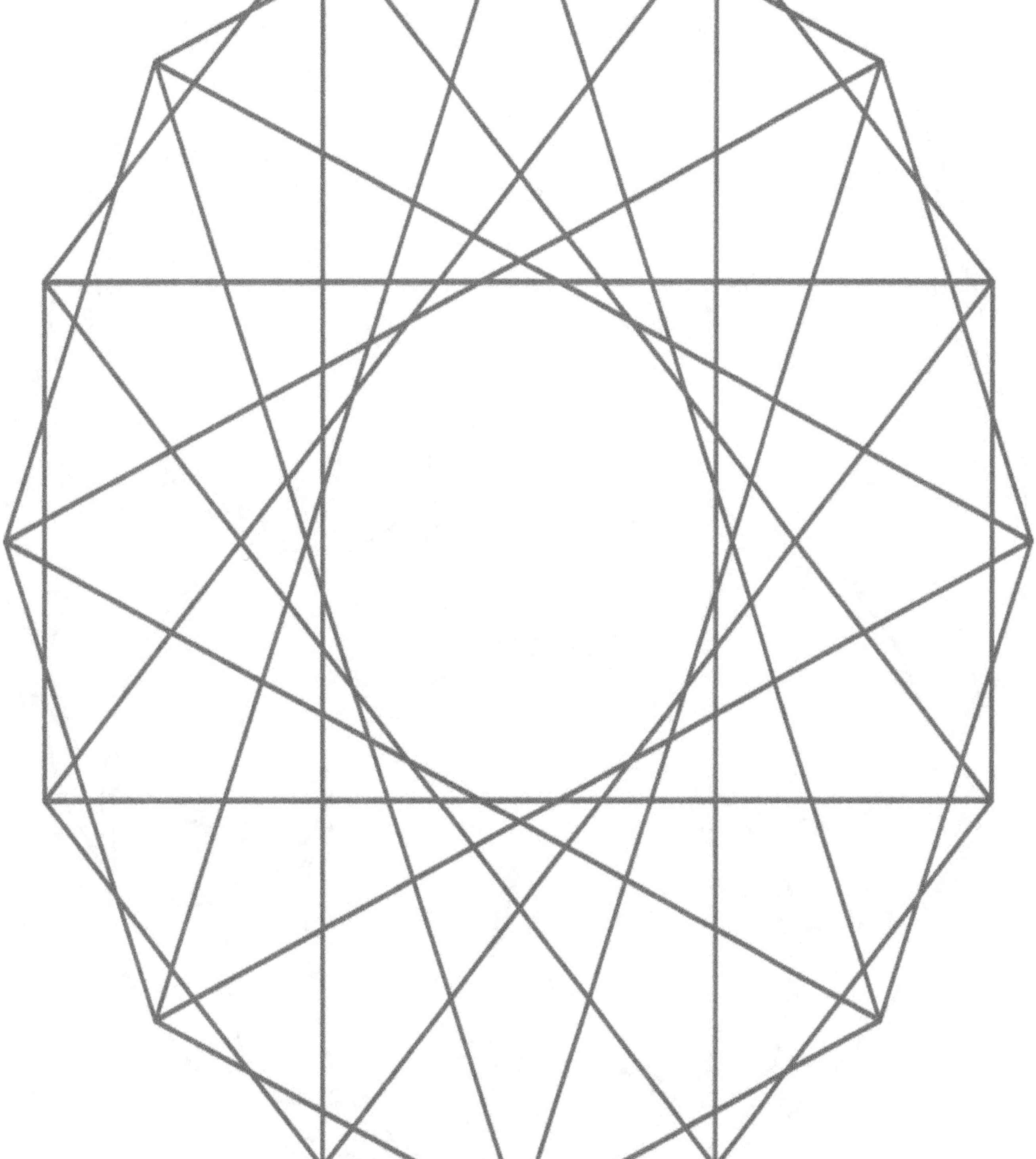

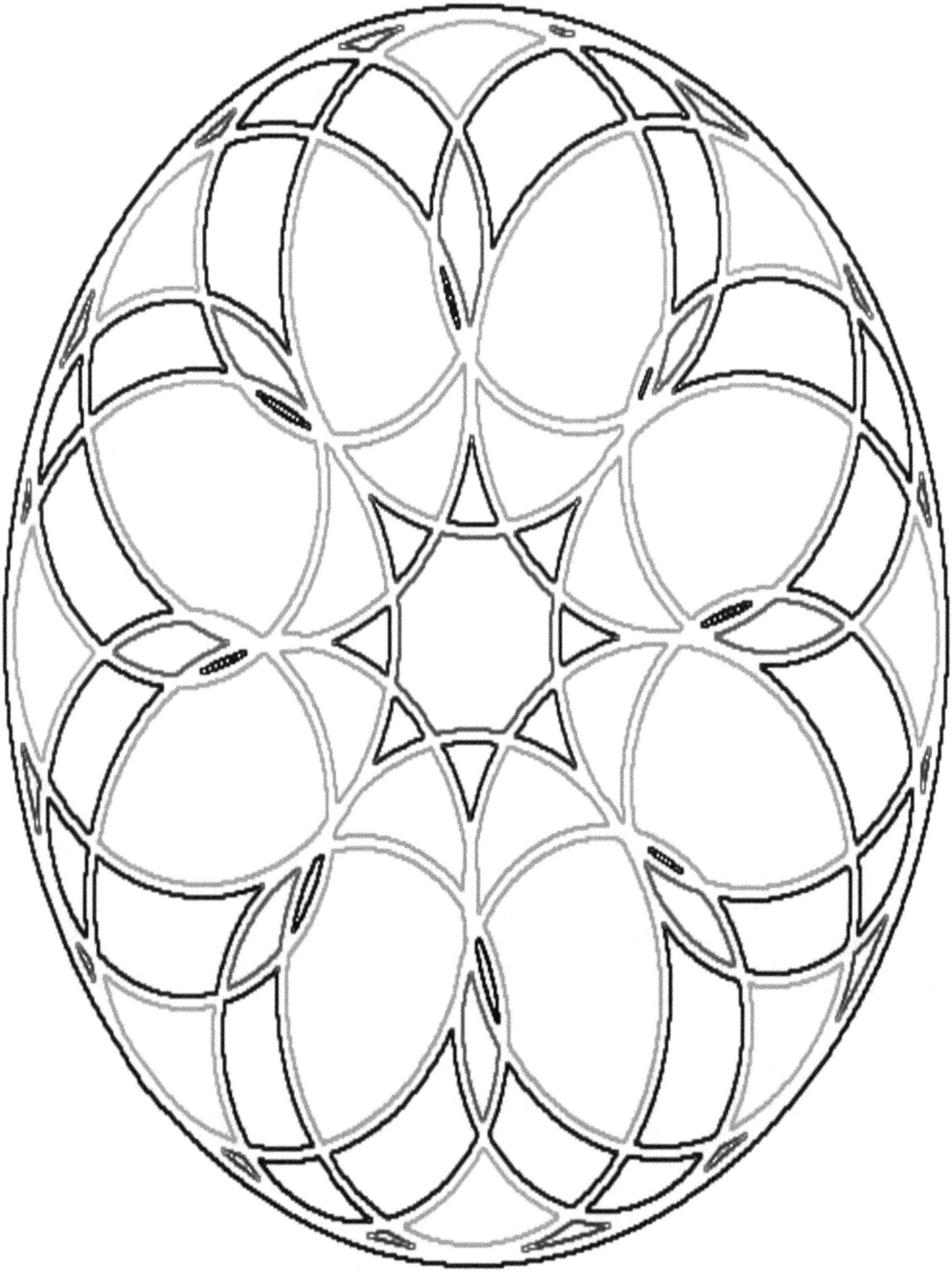

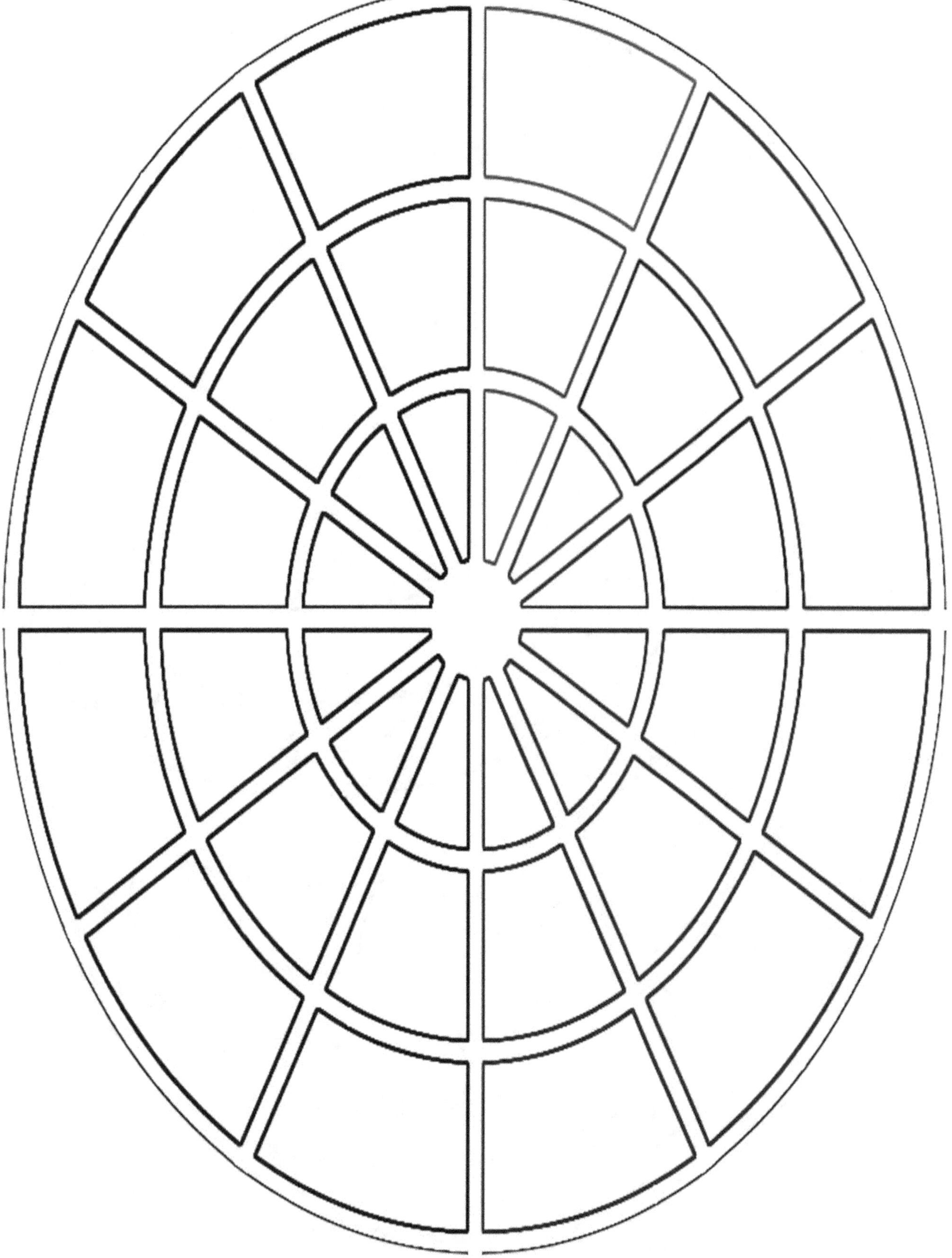

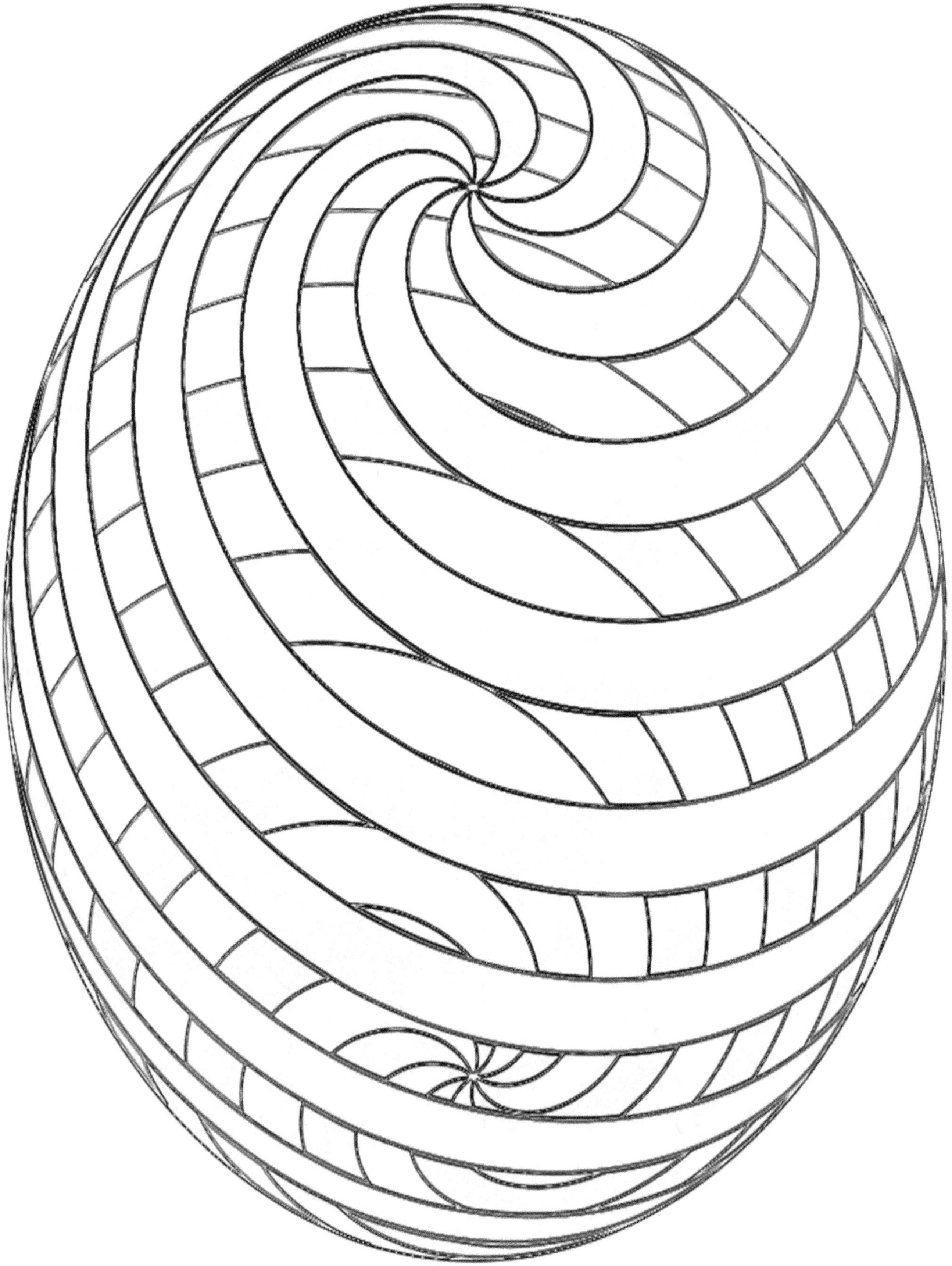

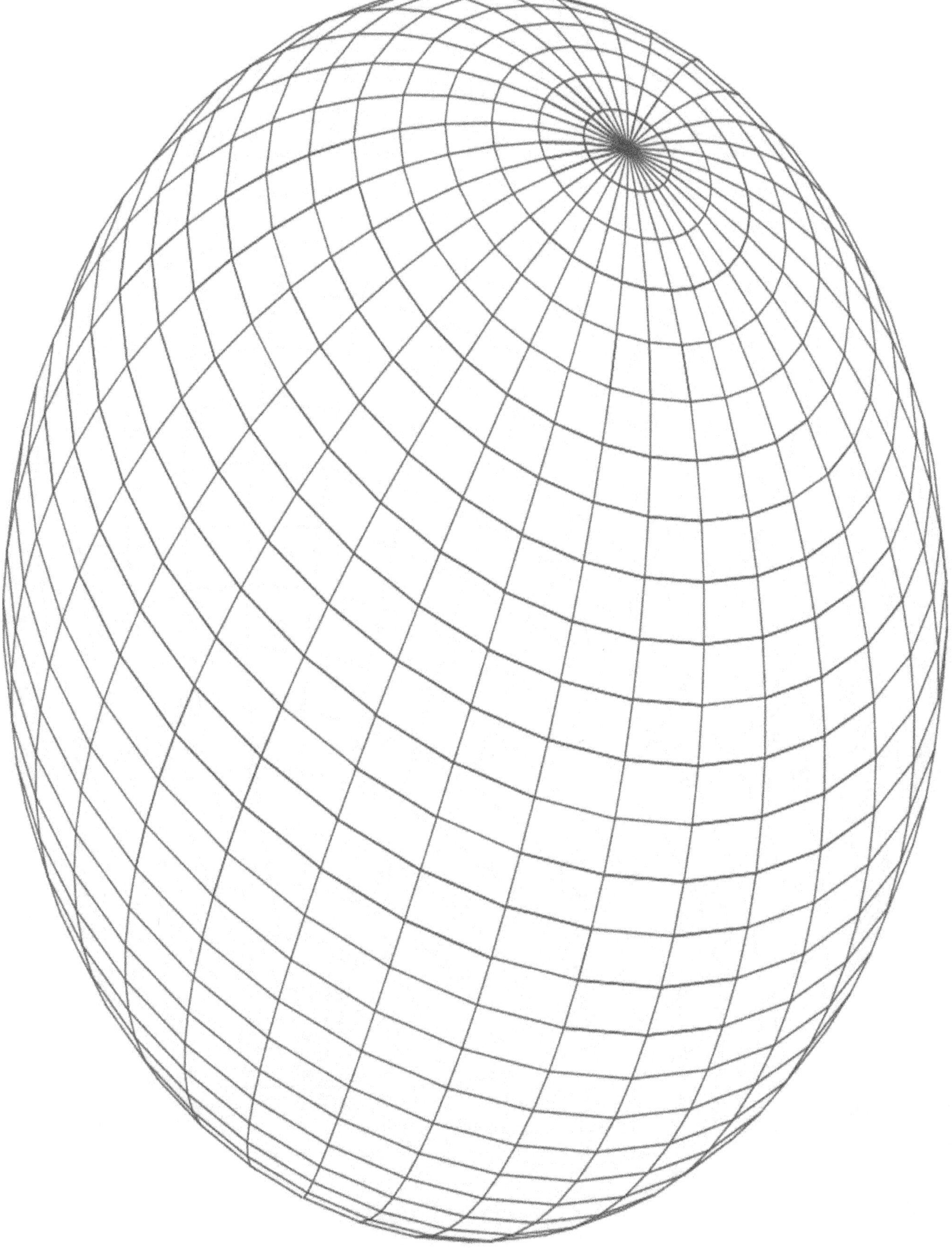

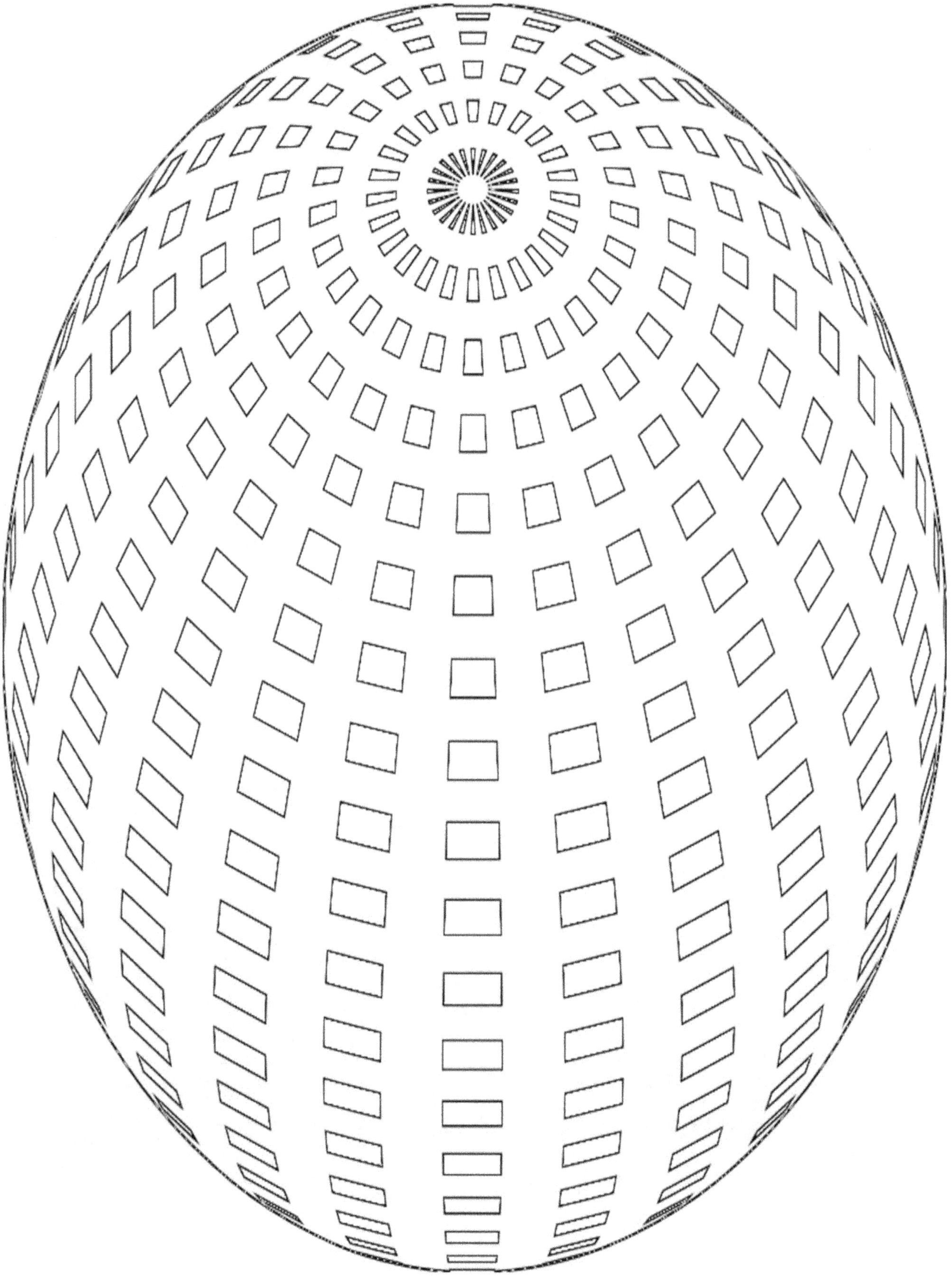

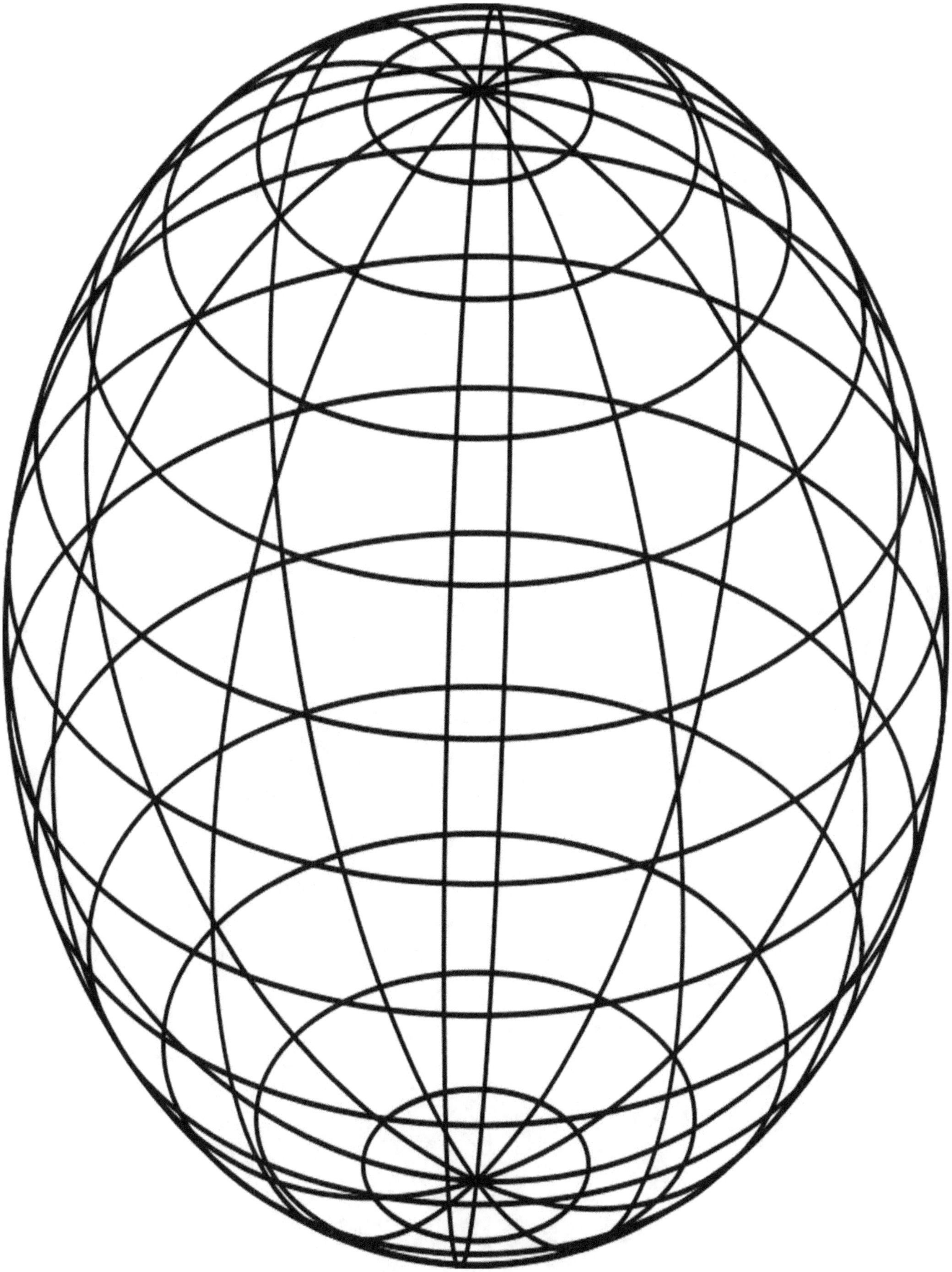

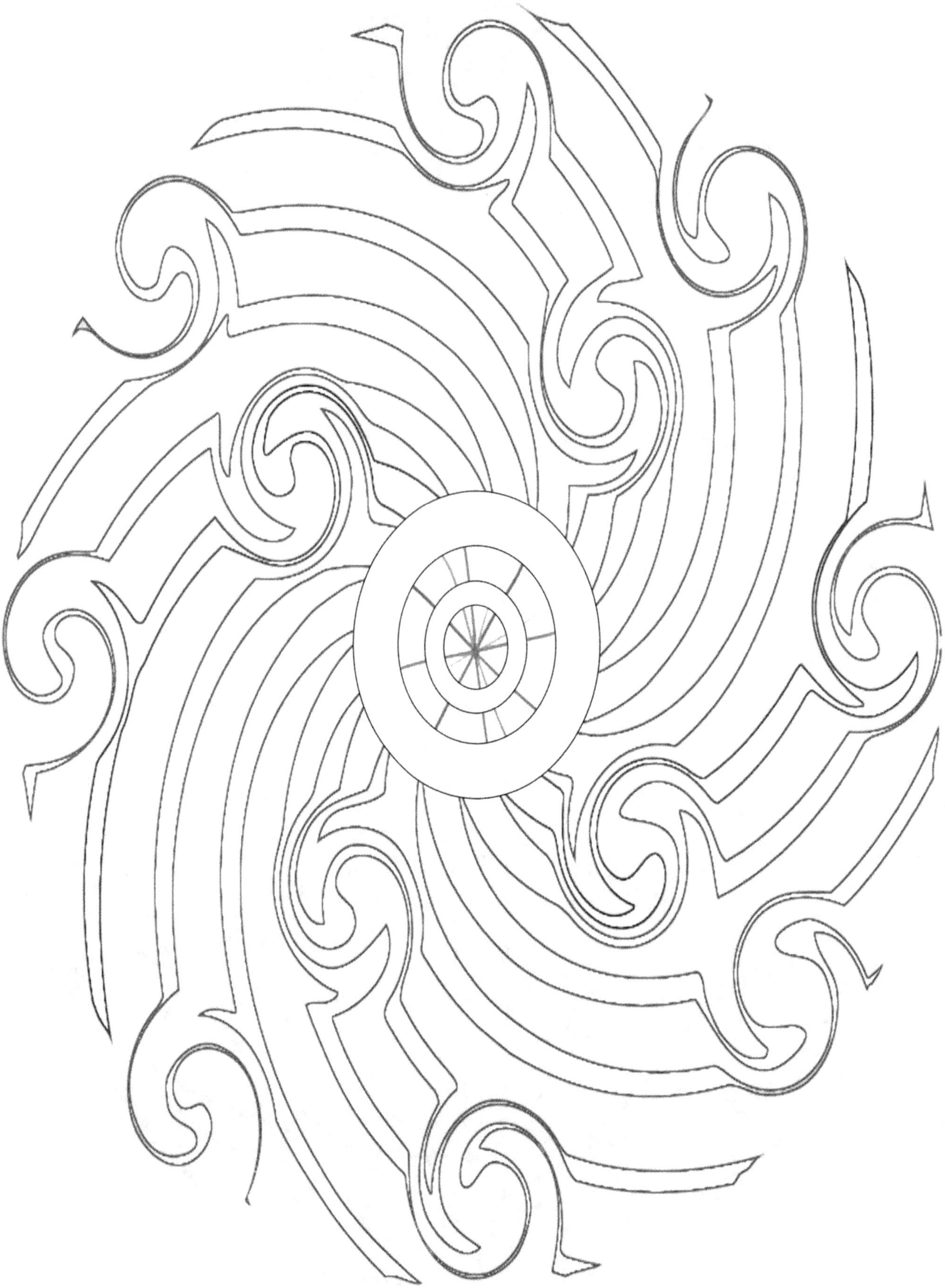

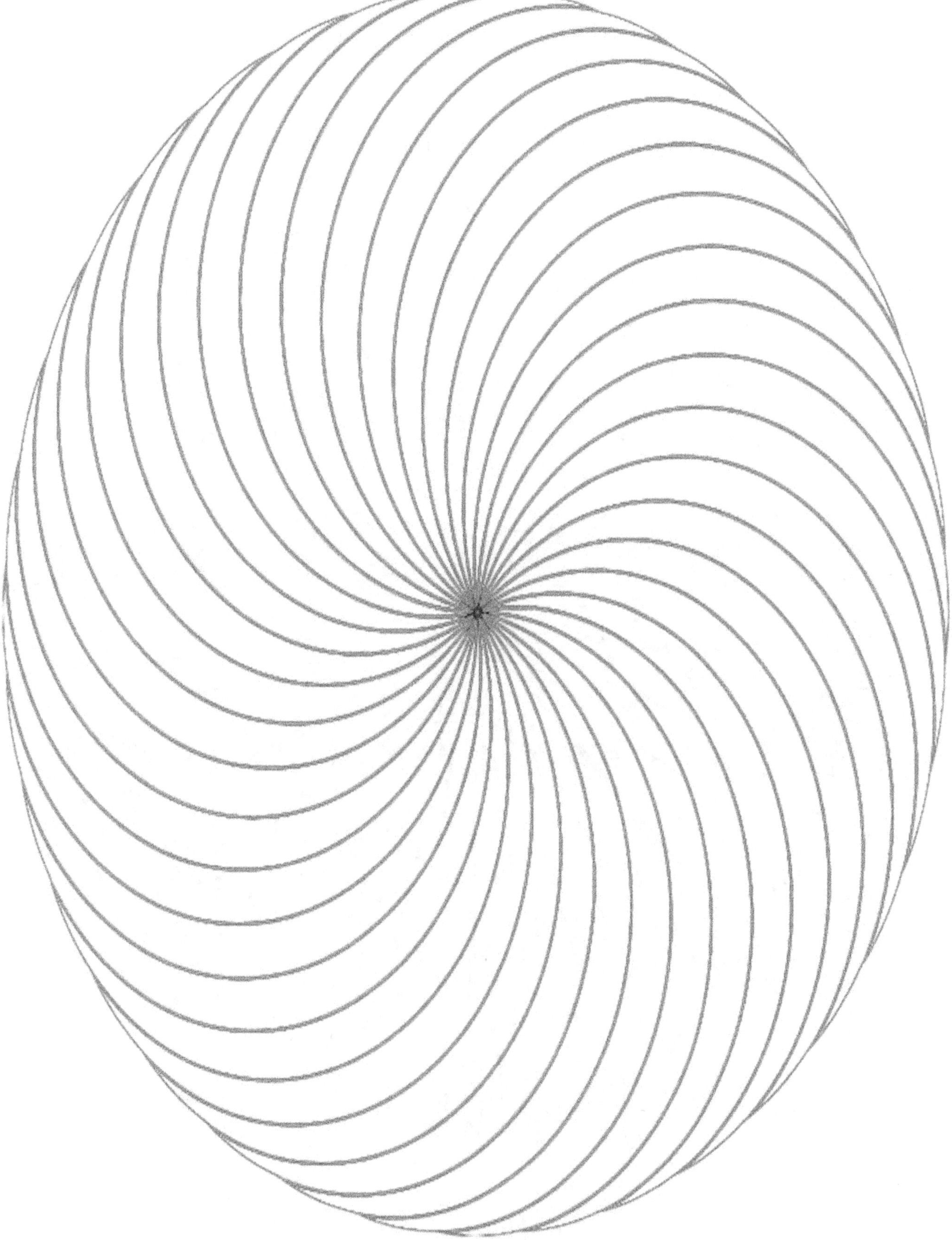

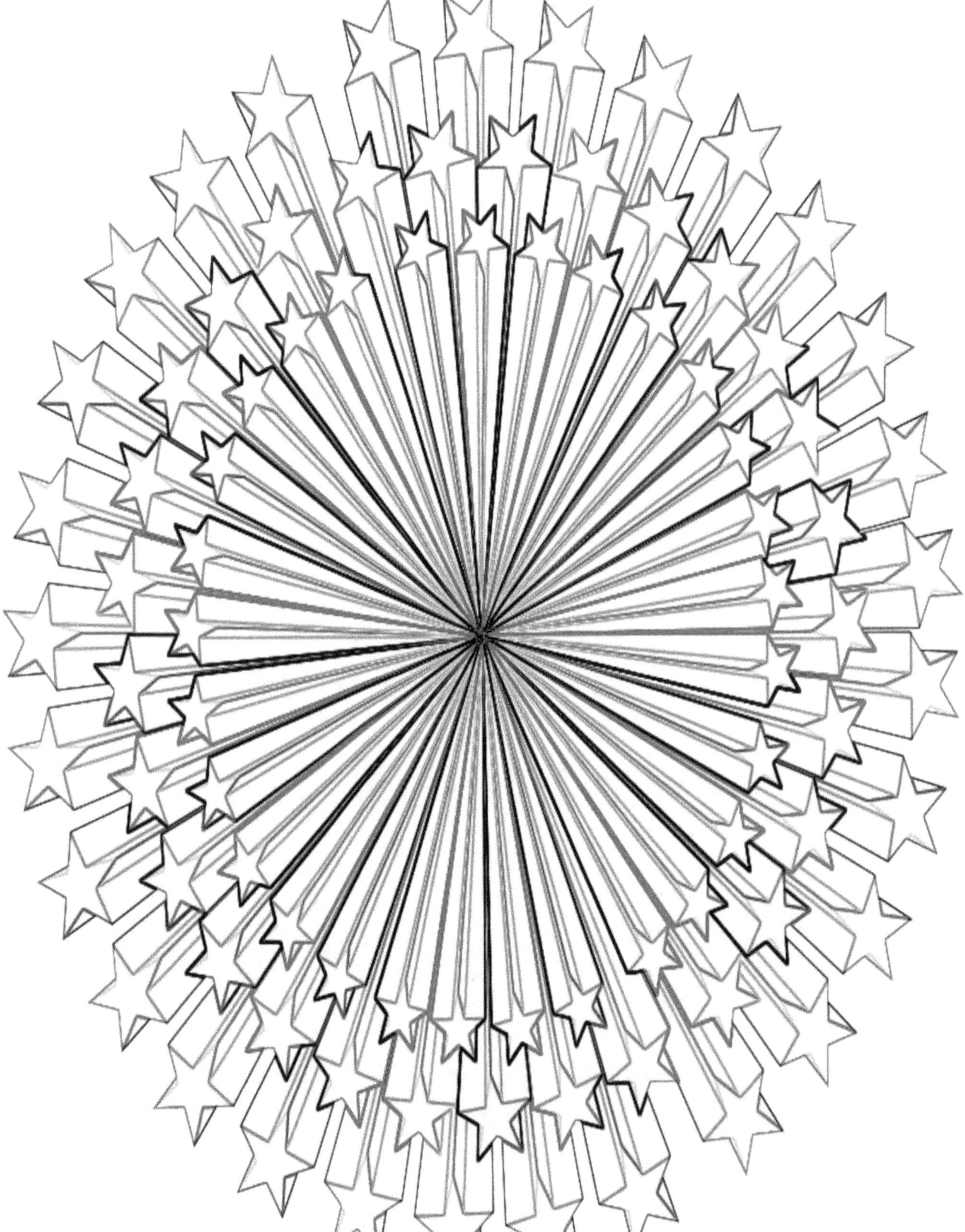

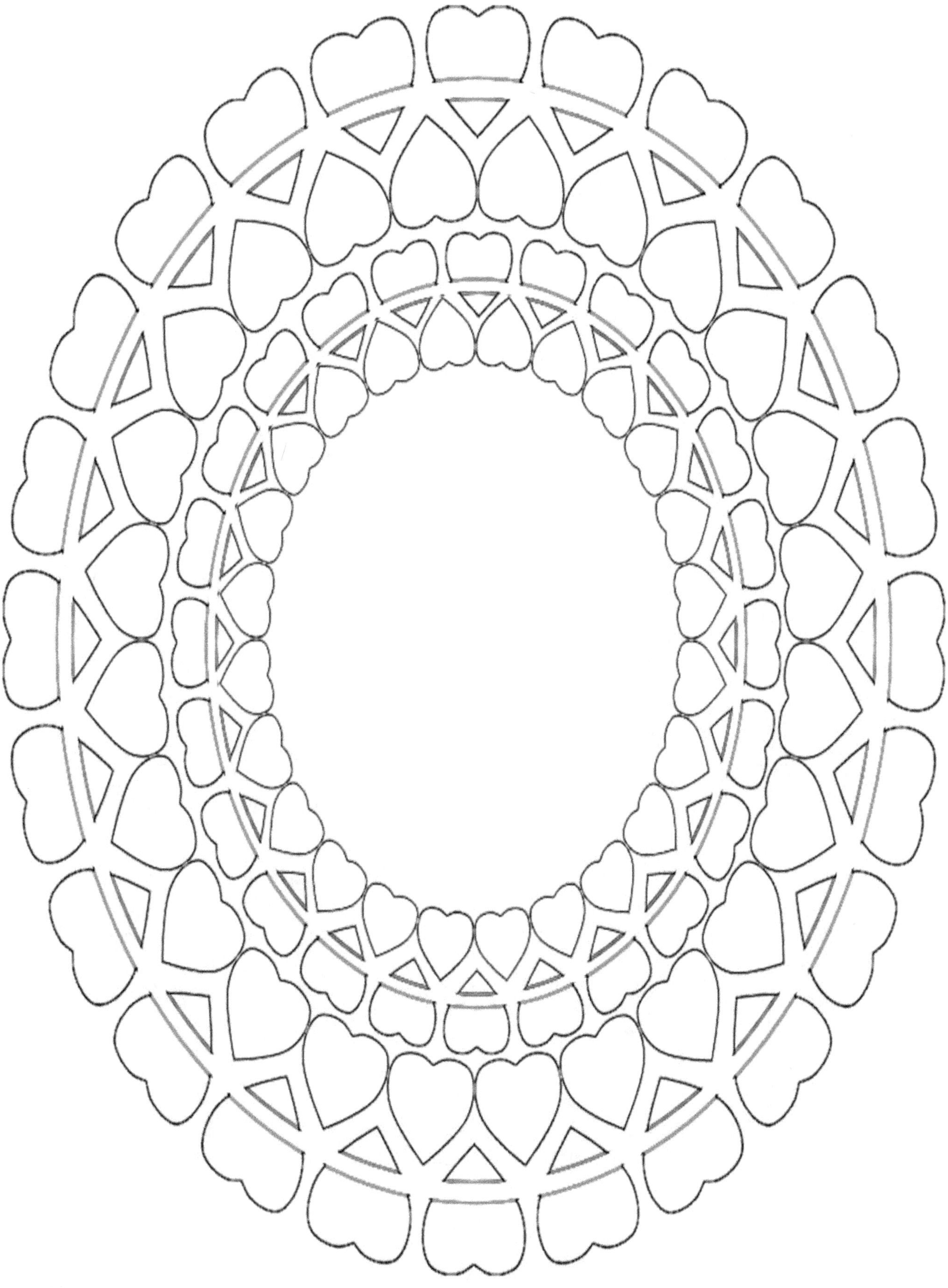

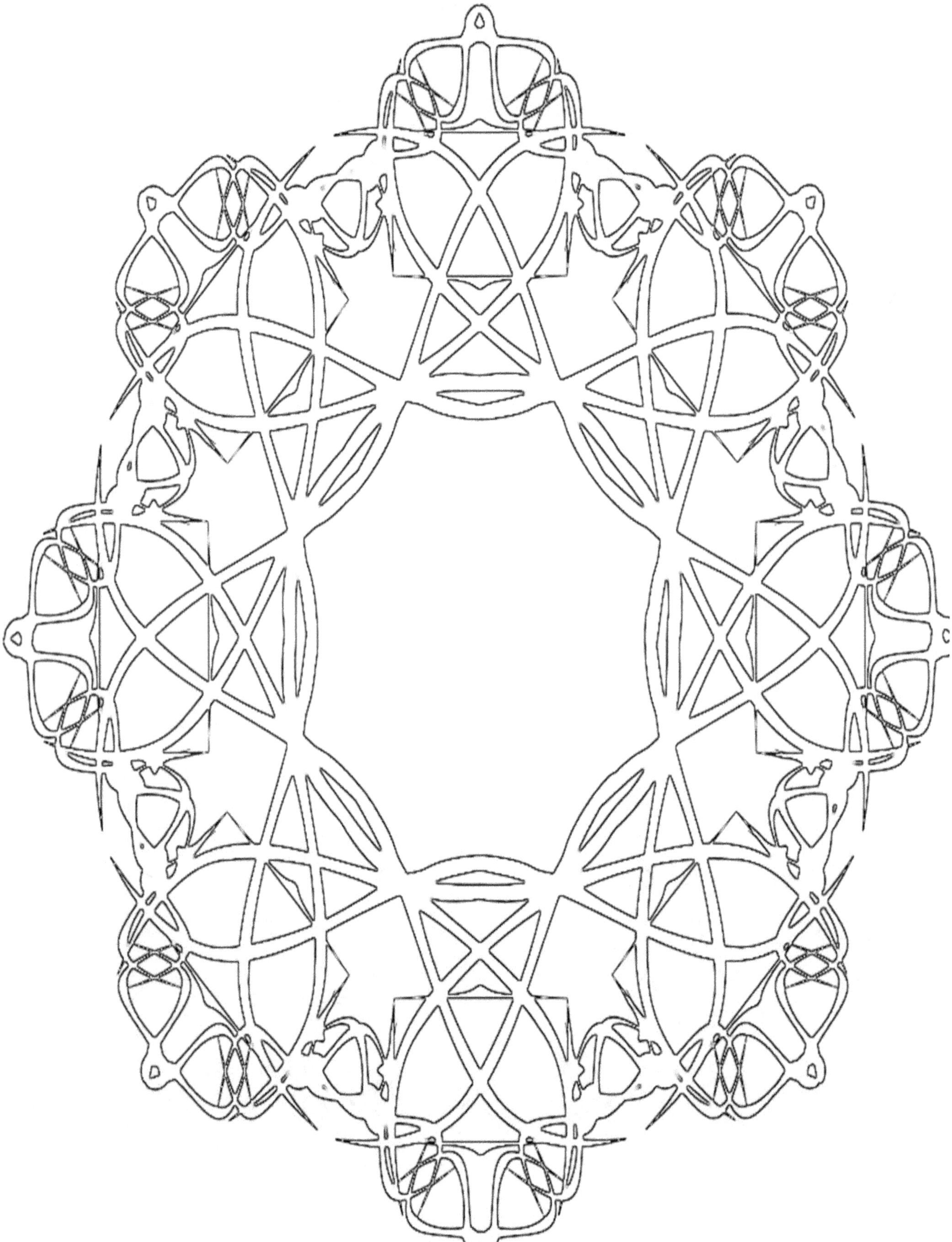

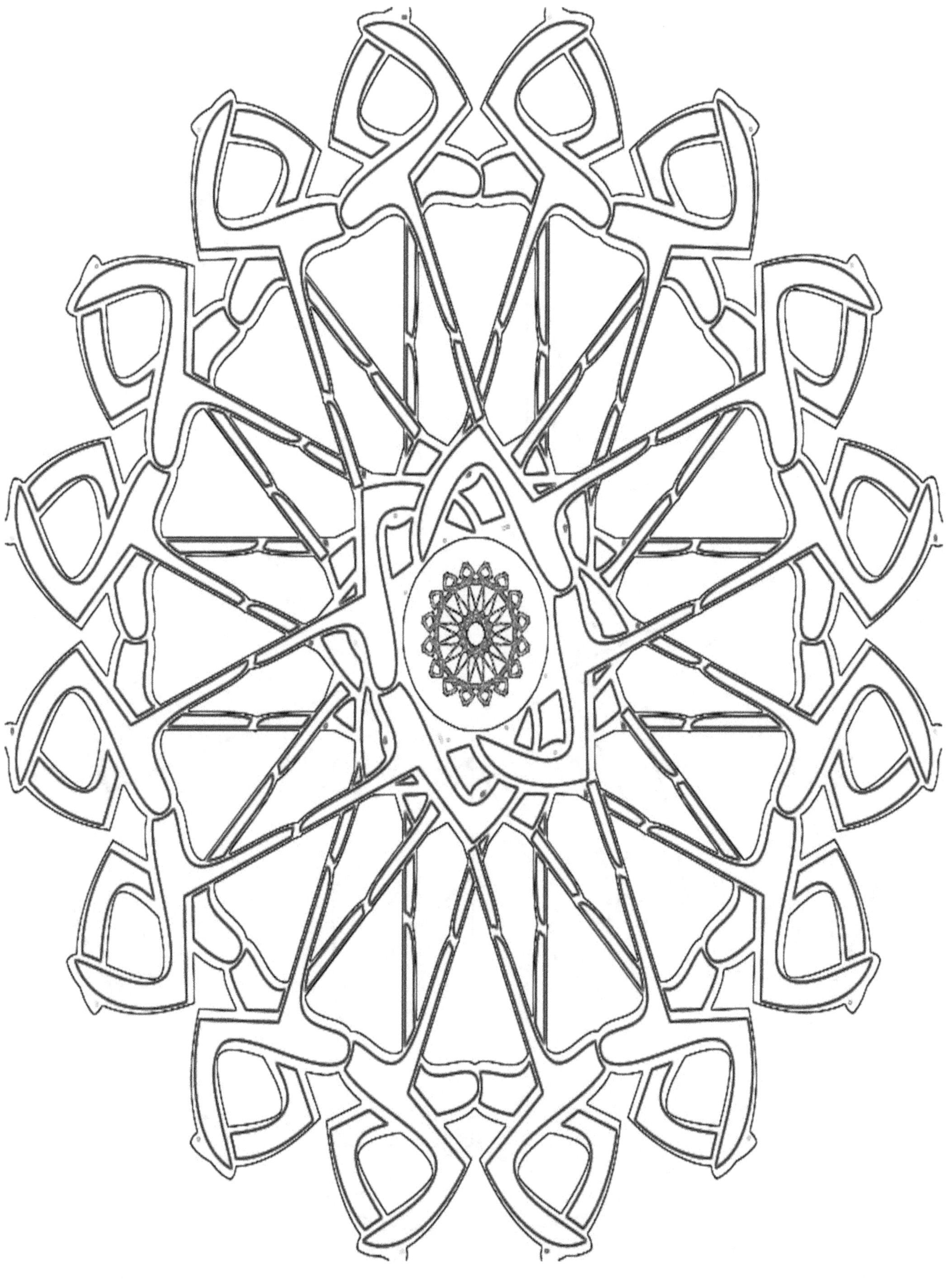

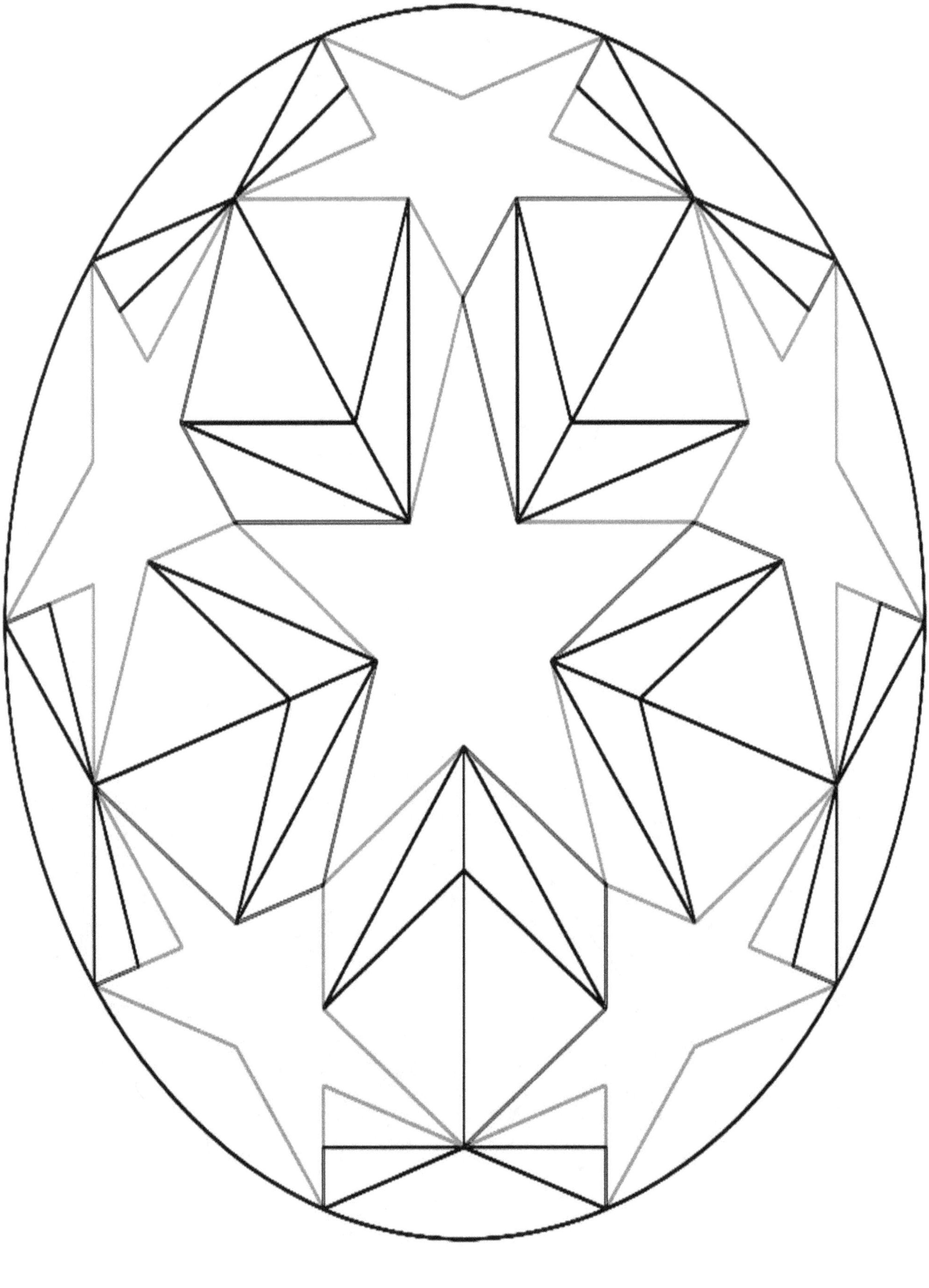

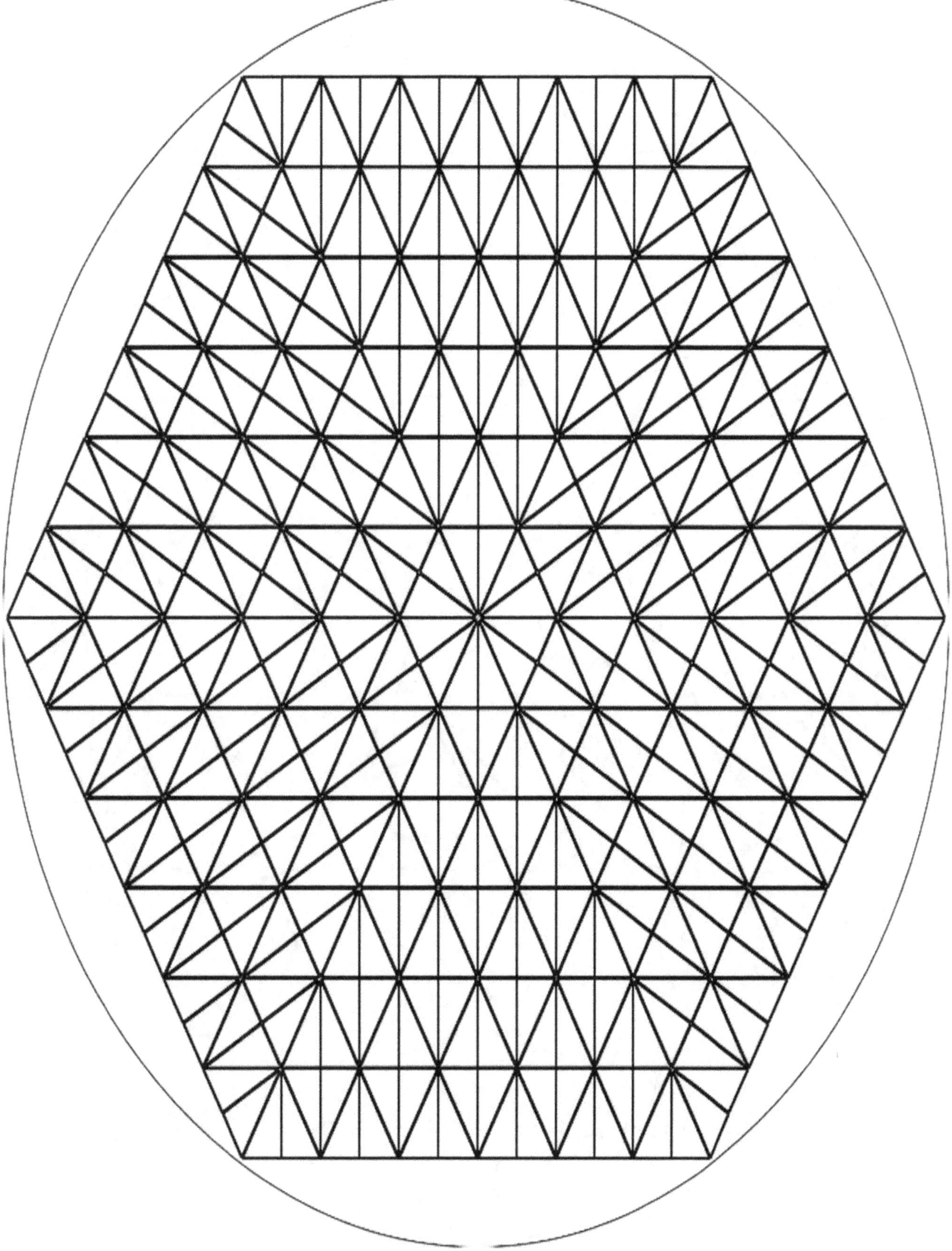

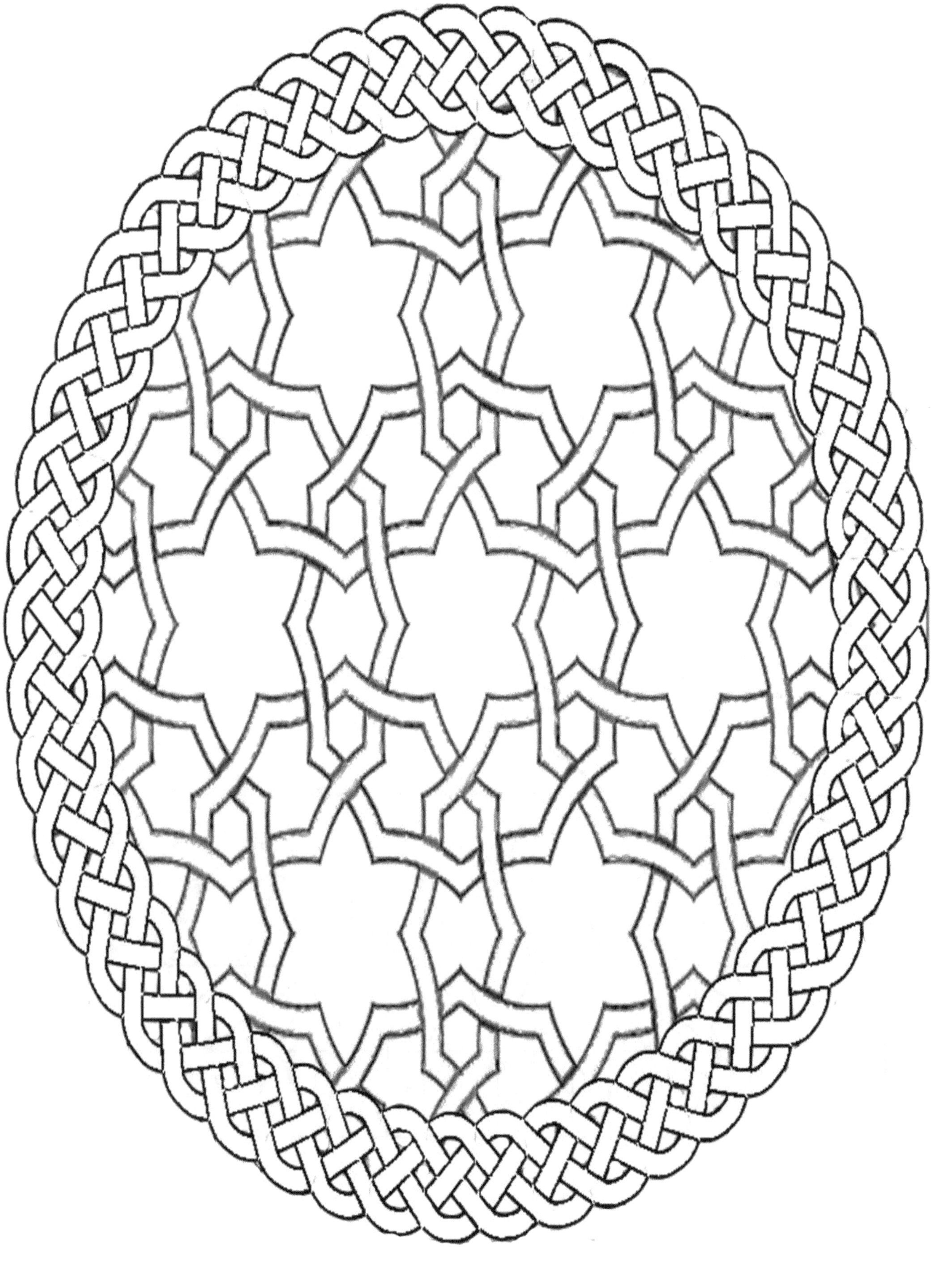

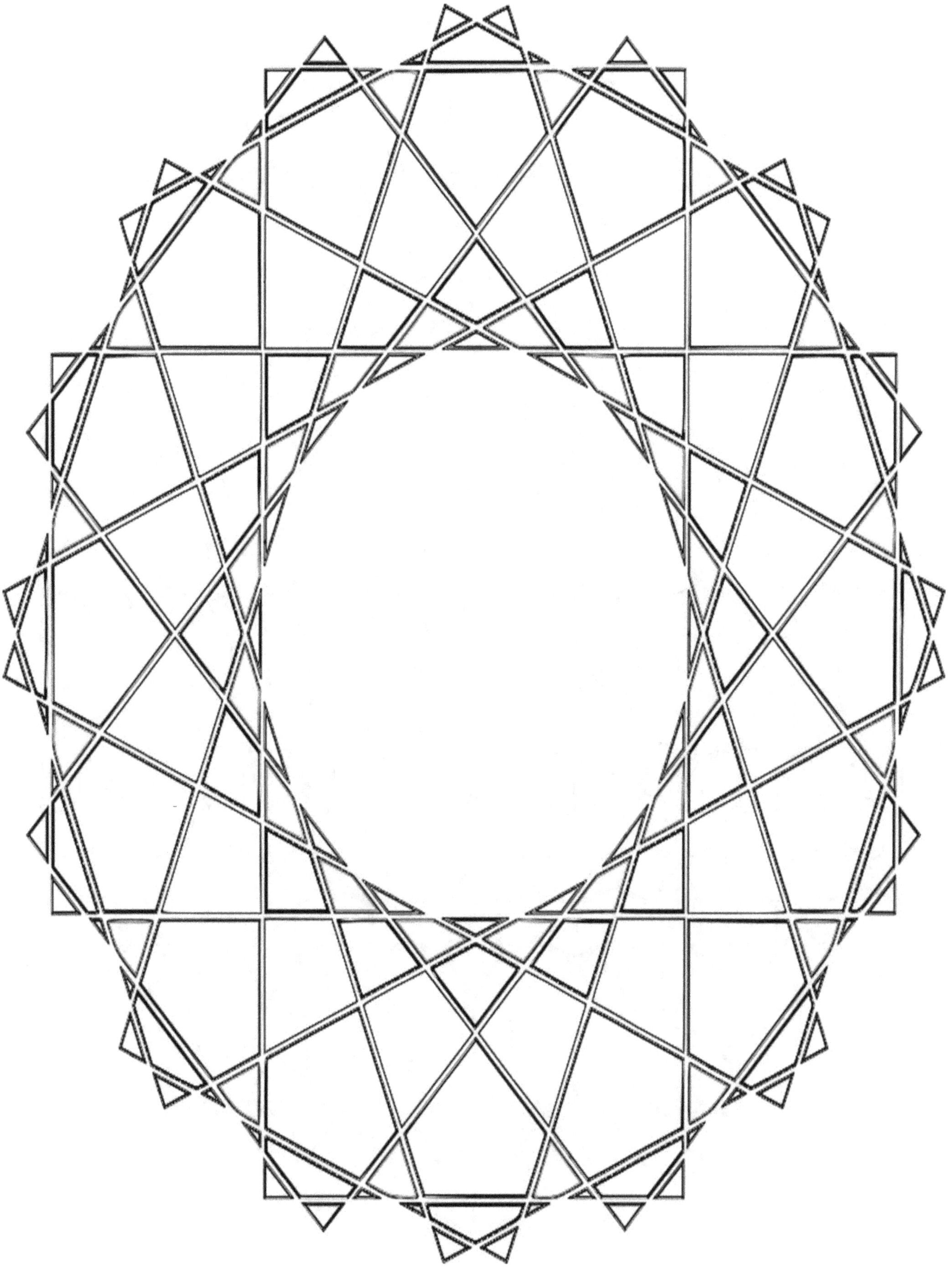

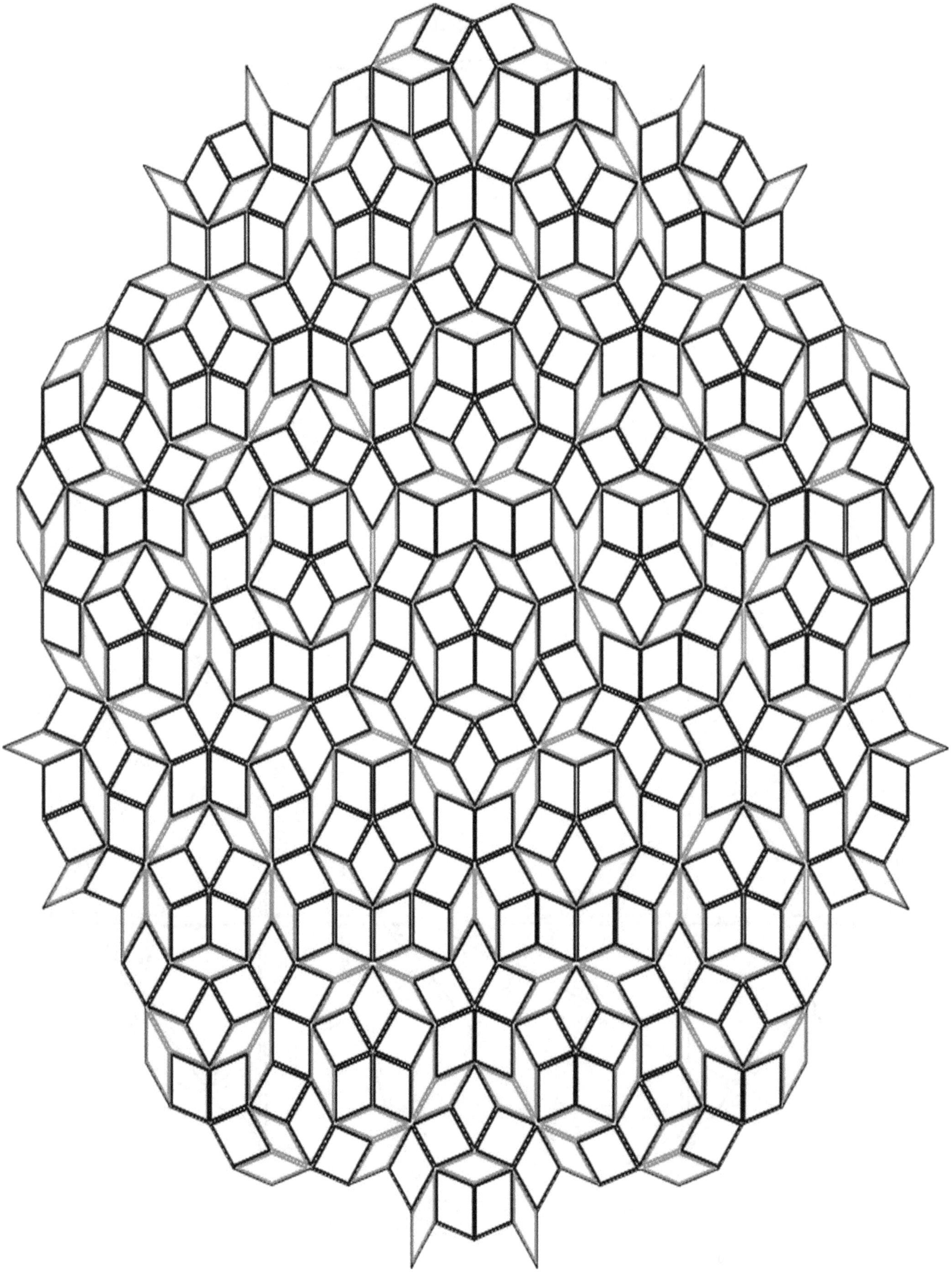

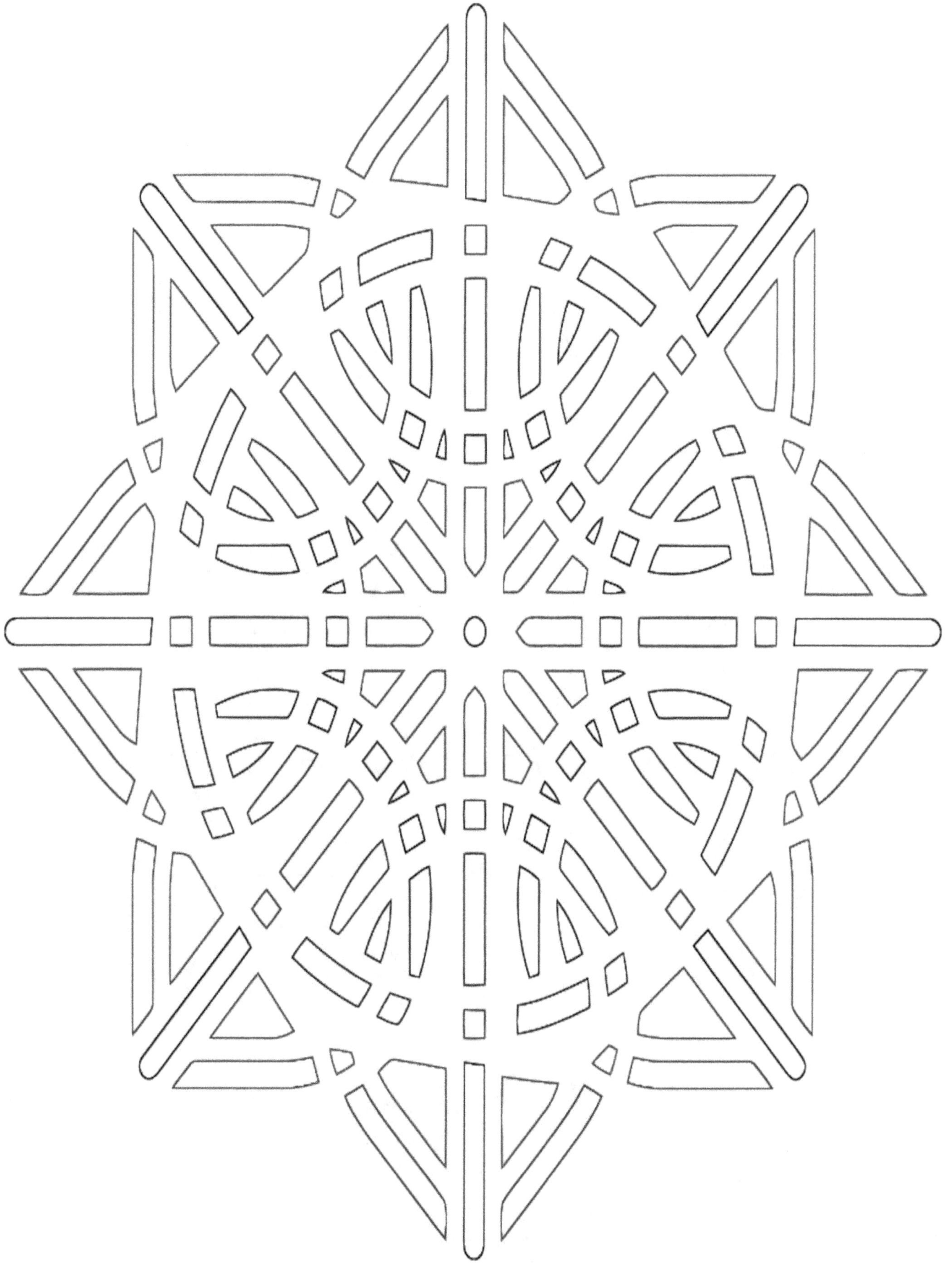

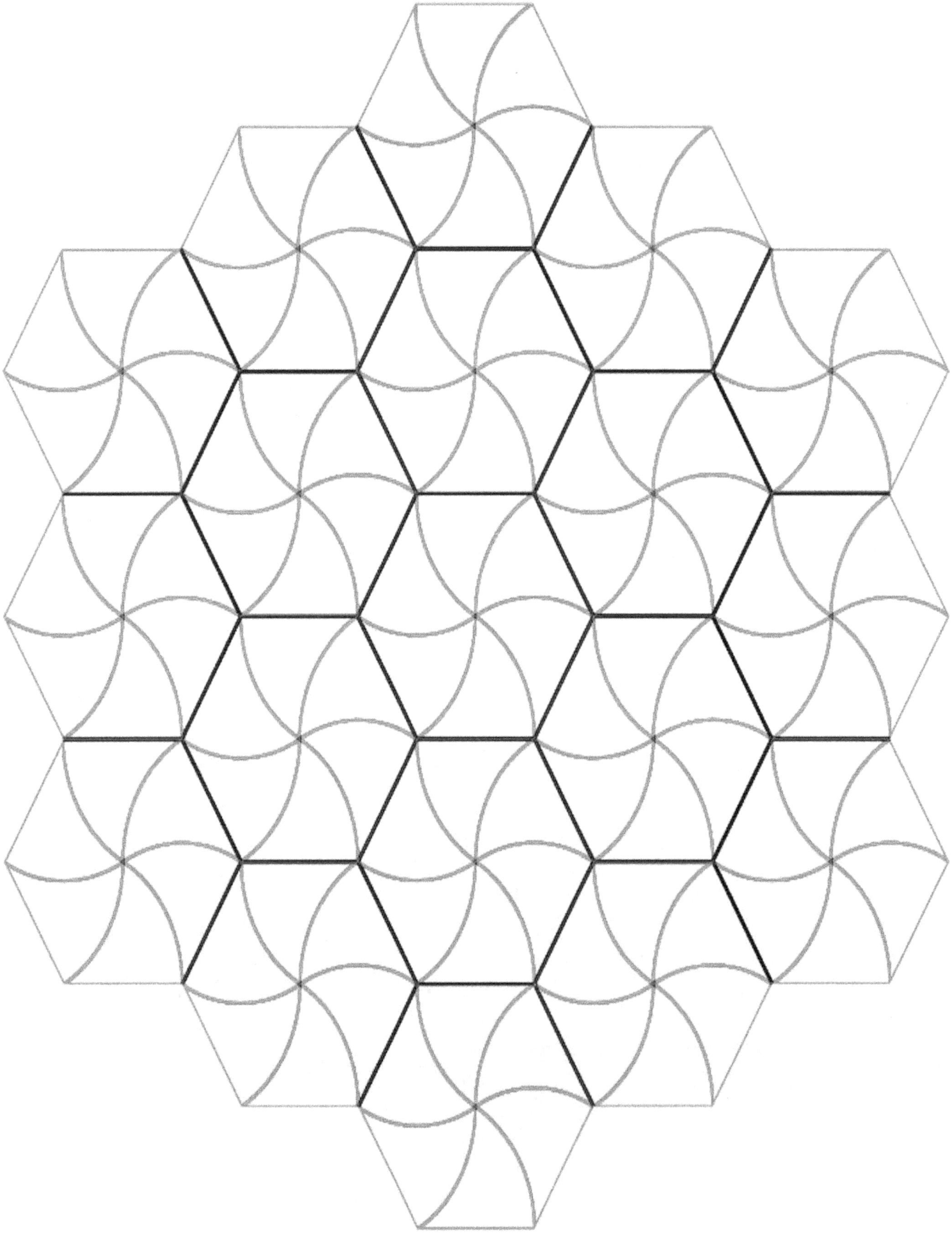

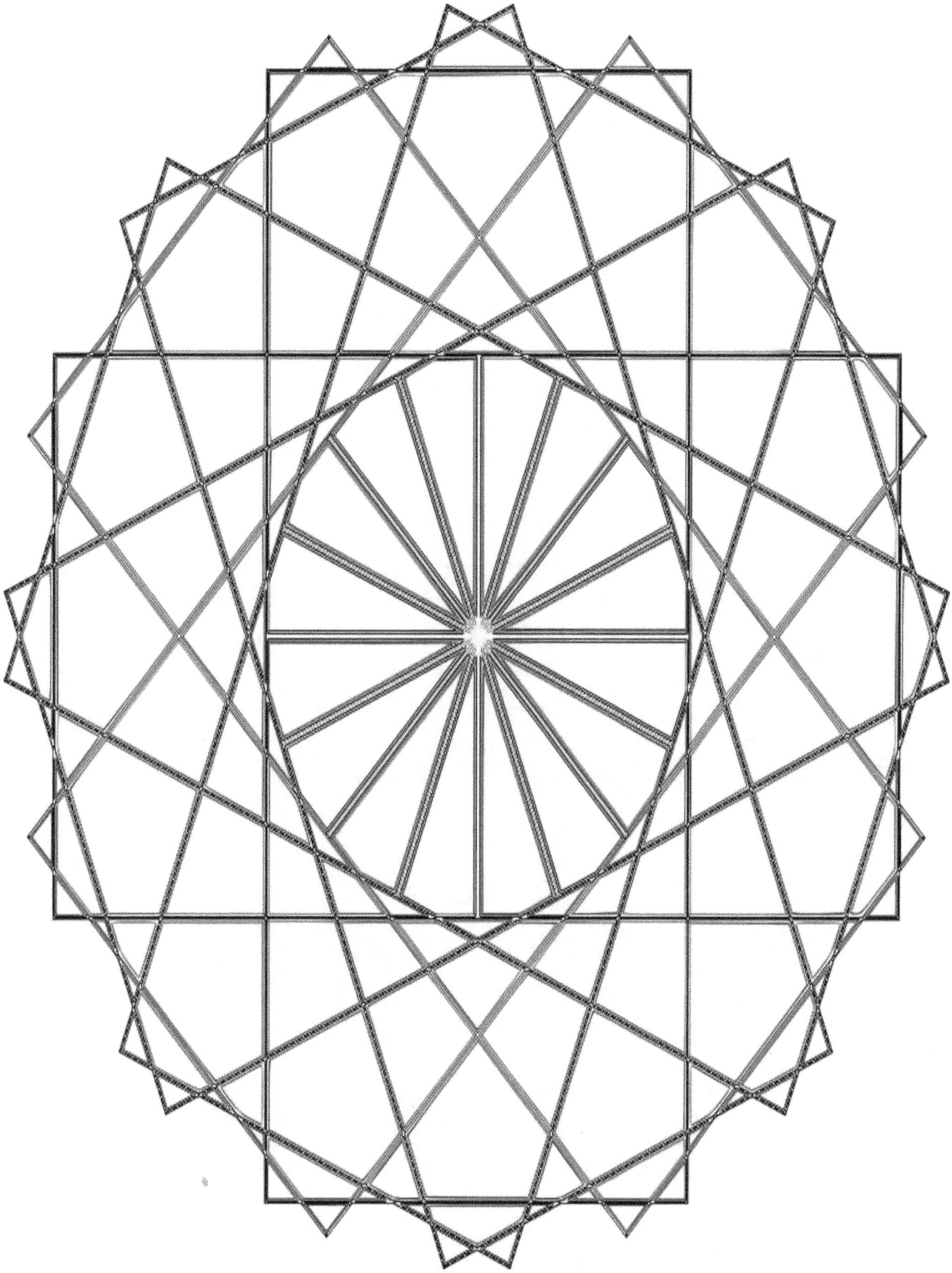

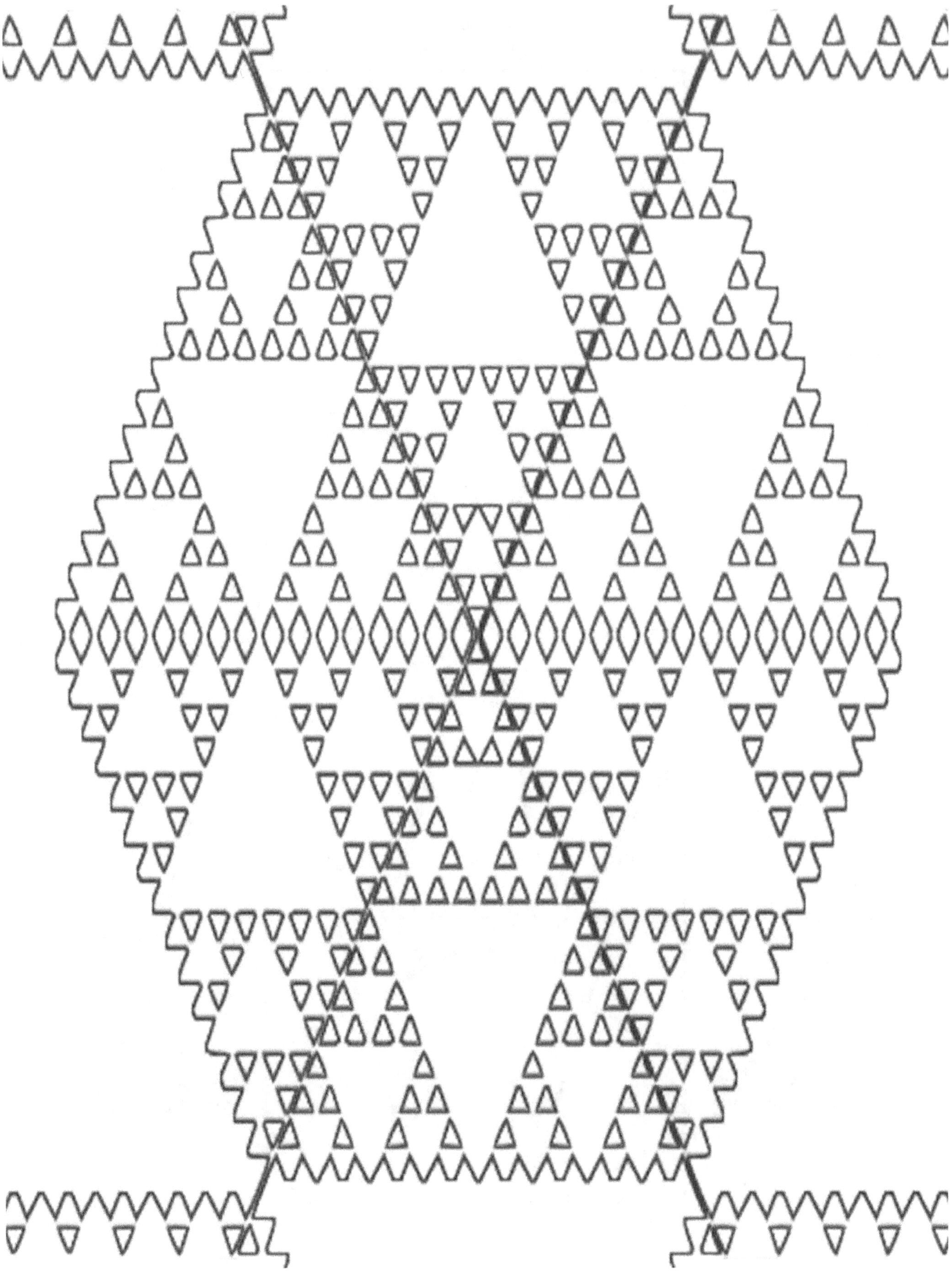

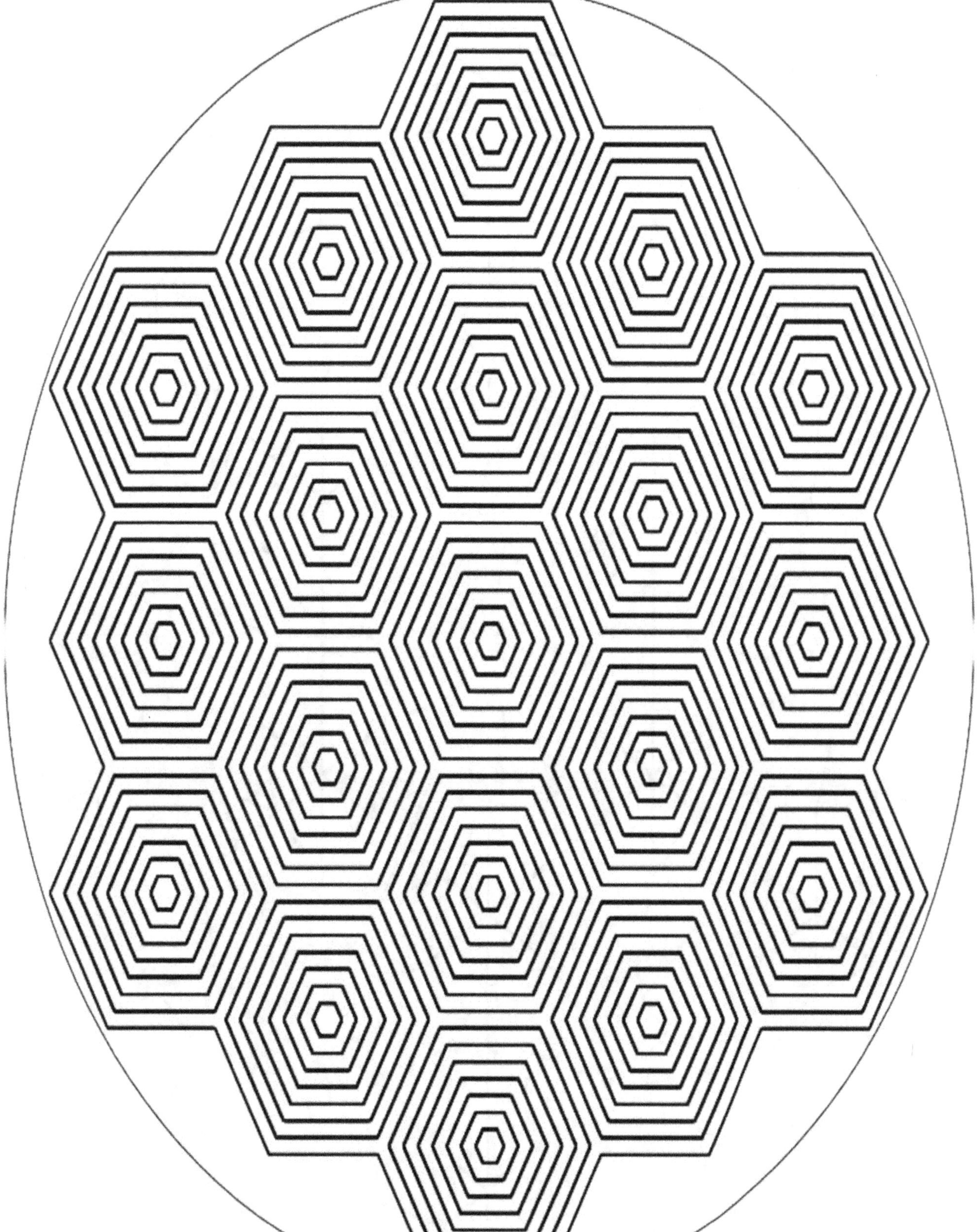

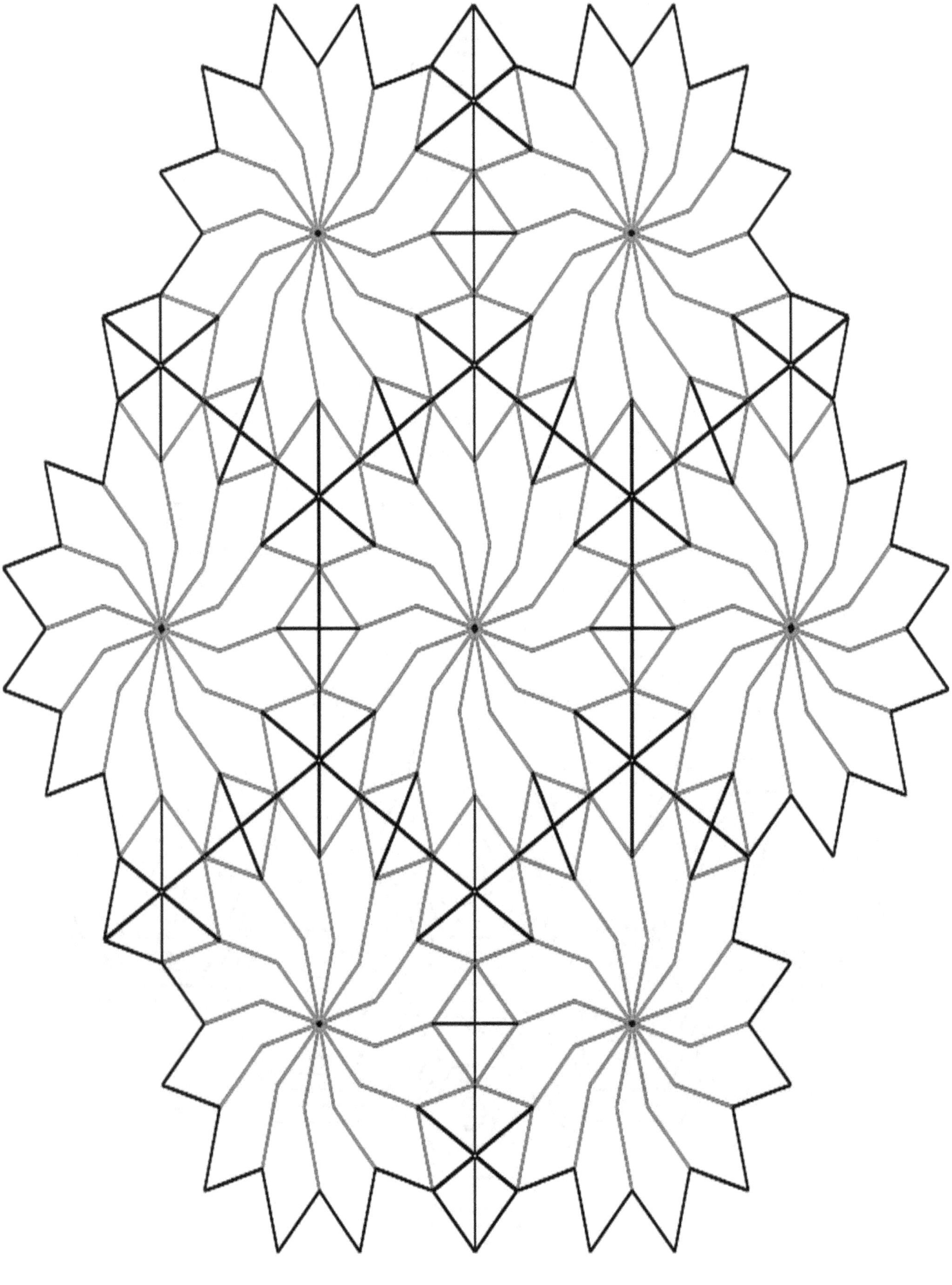

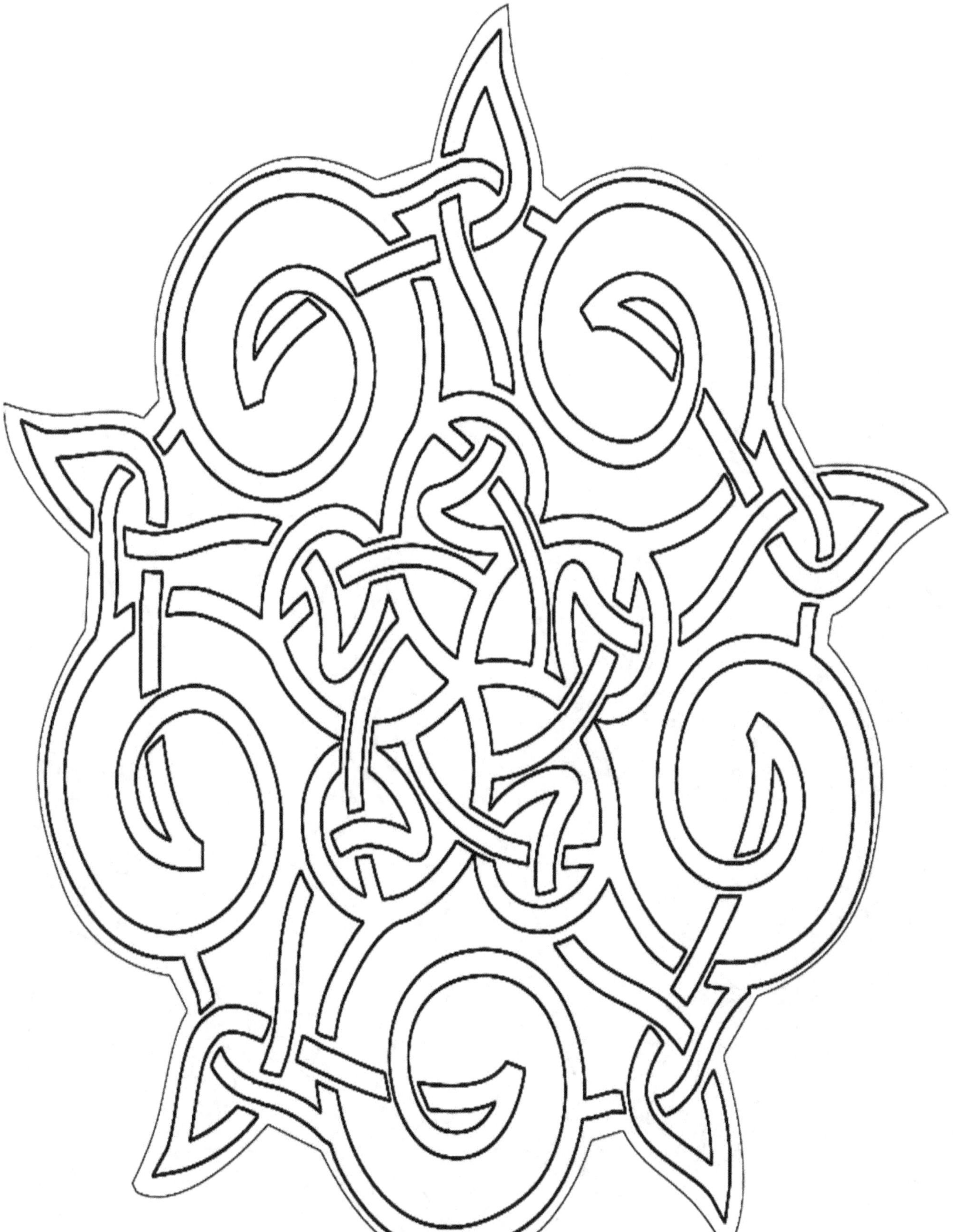

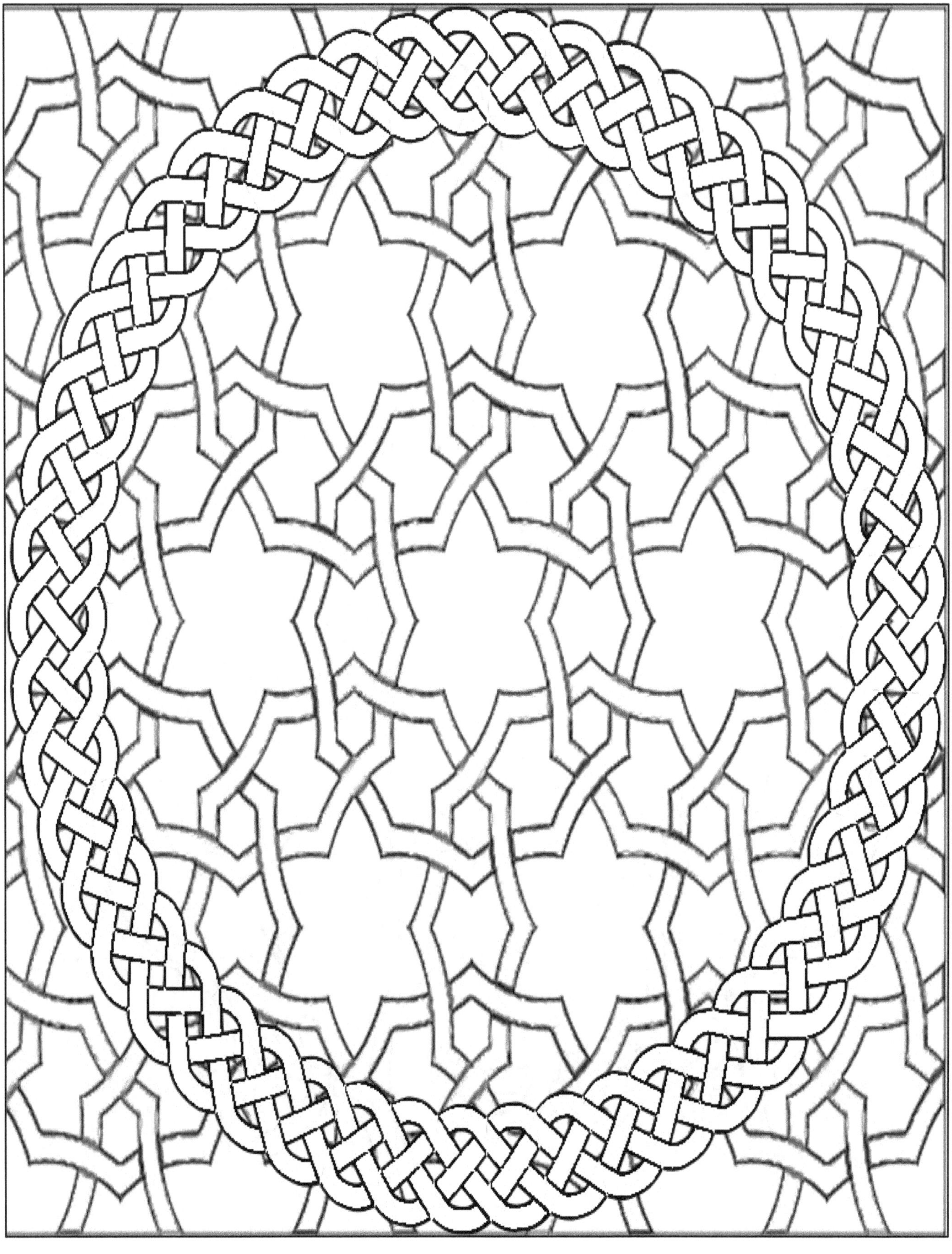

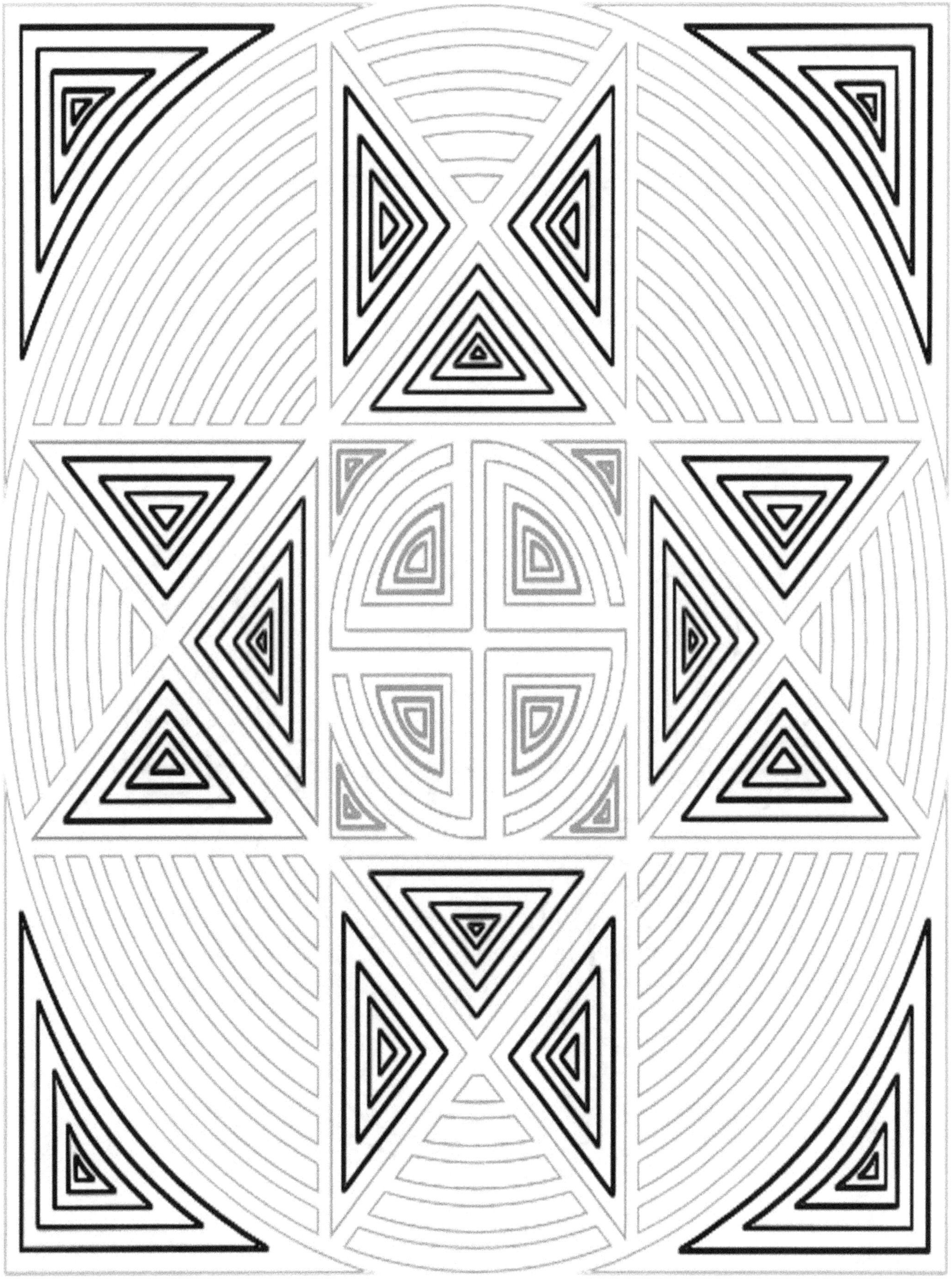

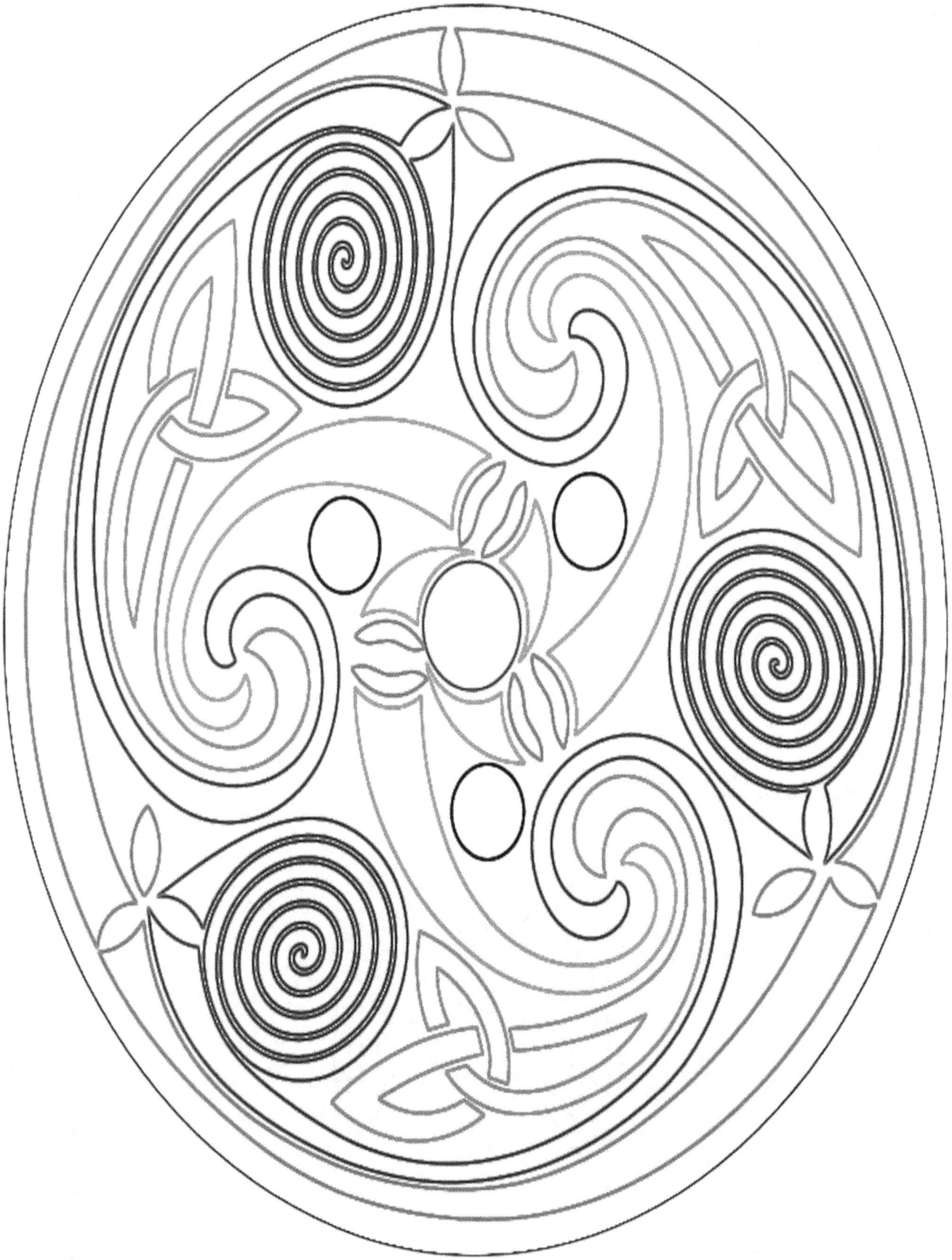

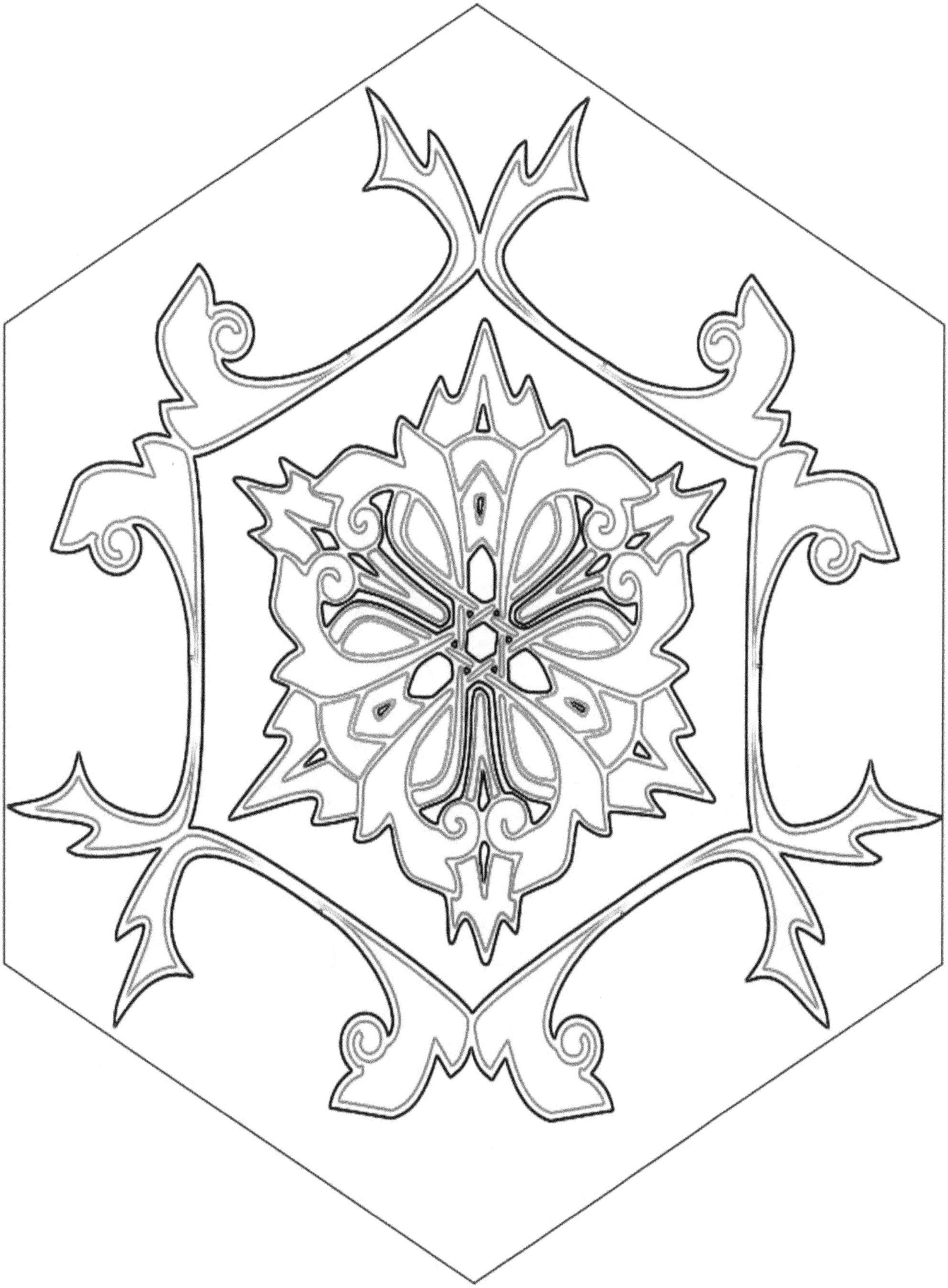

www.ingramcontent.com/pod-product-compliance
Lightning Source LLC
Chambersburg PA
CBHW080618180526
45168CB00007B/2964
* 9 7 8 1 5 1 1 9 9 6 7 7 8 *